DESIGN METHODOLOGY

DESIGN METHODOLOGY

Theoretical Fundamentals

LUZ DEL CARMEN VILCHIS ESQUIVEL

Library of Congress Control Number:		2014915882
ISBN:	Hardcover	978-1-4633-9178-2
	Softcover	978-1-4633-9179-9
	eBook	978-1-4633-9180-5

Vilchis Esquivel, Luz del Carmen
Design Methodology. Theoretical Fundamentals
1st. English Edition

Design. Methodology. Theory.

1st. English Edition

Credits
Postgraduate Program
Faculty of Arts and Design
National Autonomous University of Mexico
Iconography
Ti Kip Fernández Vilchis (q.e.p.d.)
Cover Image
Leonardo da Vinci.
Double manuscript page on the
Sforza Monument.
(Public Domain)

This book was printed in the United States of America.

Rev. date: 30/10/2014

To order additional copies of this book, contact:
Palibrio
1663 Liberty Drive
Suite 200
Bloomington, IN 47403
Toll Free from the U.S.A 877.407.5847
Toll Free from Mexico 01.800.288.2243
Toll Free from Spain 900.866.949
From other International locations +1.812.671.9757
Fax: 01.812.355.1576
orders@palibrio.com
669997

TO MY DEAR AND
BELOVED DAUGHTER.
TI FERNÁNDEZ VILCHIS
(1982-2014)
REST IN PEACE

CONTENTS

INTRODUCTION

"Truth is not a copy. It is not a sign
nor a mental reflection. It is something we make
in the encounter with the world that is making us"
Marshall McLuhan

This book is aimed at students and teachers in design degrees and researchers interested in logical thinking on design. Just like any other discipline, design must accredit its rational fundamentals, which is why it is necessary to refer to the ontological principles in which it lies and conditions of knowledge that determine it as a specific object of study. In virtue of this, methodology serves as a bridge between the general principles of doing and of knowing - which are common to every knowledge - and the specific subject characteristics.

Given that the methodology determines the particular universes of knowledge, the analysis of the theoretic fundamentals of design involves an approach to its methodological models – according to the manner in which they have been exhibited by their authors -, as well as the general principles of the methodology and the conceptual assumptions in which they lie. Likewise, it establishes the indissoluble relationship between theory, method and technique, that thinking and doing present in their necessary unit.

The approach makes necessary not only the remission to philosophical principles, but also taking a standpoint that, faced with these principles, forces all true praxis.

The exhibited methodological principles make evident the interdisciplinary nature that is inevitable in the theory and practice of design, which also supposes axiological considerations – taking into account the epistemological and the ontological – whereas, as in any human creation, design has a sense and a social function that are inherent to it and which cannot be alien to someone for whom design is an object of study or a professional practice.

The approach presented herein exhibits design as a discipline and a making integrated in the social environment because, as any human making, it cannot be untied of its conditioning factors nor of its social consequences. The perspective allows understanding design in it fundamental aspects, inevitably controversial.

The study's critical content springs from the objective analysis of the theories as well as the methodological models, with strict attachment to the theses of their authors and to the concepts that serve as a connecting thread, without implying any judgment regarding their functioning.

The immediate objective of this work is to provide a starting point that is open to different theoretic possibilities and different technical alternatives, as well as to subsequent researches, in both the strictly philosophical field as well as in the practice of which necessity is manifested, due to the scarce specialized literature that is written in Mexico on design. This work also has as its objective to establish conceptual links between design and all the branches of knowledge related to object communication.

METHODOLOGY

Every discipline is structured based on a tripartite system of which scheme integrates theory (foundations, general rules, concepts, etc.), method (models of thought organization) and technique (practical and operative procedures). It is important to understand that in a single discipline there are as many methods as there are schools of thought, and the validity of each discipline lies in the content that is adjudged to it and in its links to the study objects.

In order to survive, man faces the need to maintain a constant relationship with the natural environment, with other human beings and with things, under the discipline of observation. Thus, nature compensates his apparent lack of morphological endowments and gives him the ability to sense and to reason: walking straight, binocular vision, a brain with more capacity and complexity, prolonged childhood within an adult collectivity, etc., are factors that favour man's capacity to do and to learn.

The opportunity to know allows man to not be indifferent to the world and consider its environment, susceptible to changes and subject to a constant process of transformation.

Knowledge carries a relationship between the subject who knows and the object that is known, in which the first, to a certain degree, appropriates the last. In this process, the conditions of the subject who knows form part of the process of knowledge, and so knowledge must be understood as an historical, evolutional process. Braunstein proposes distinguishing between the sensible or sensorial knowledge of the objects and the objective knowledge that results of a rupture with what is sensible, of a criticism of appearances and of the ideas that, in a more or less spontaneous manner, we make of things; a criticism, at the end, of what historical materialism calls ideology.

It is convenient to explain, due to the diversity of meanings of the term ideology, that for Braunstein it consists of the pre-scientific knowledge. Knowledge regarding the apparent movement is the acknowledgement of the manner in which things appear and ignorance regarding the structure that their appearance produces.

> [...] it is the indispensable step prior to the construction of a scientific theory. Between the ideological knowing and the scientific knowledge there is a clear breach (epistemological rupture) but there is also an indissoluble relation that links them and reciprocally implicates them.[1]

---

1 Néstor A. Braunstein, *Psychology, Ideology and Science*, p. 11

There are other factors in addition to the ideological ones, such as observation and experience, without which there would be no scientific knowledge; but these elements by themselves cannot determine the conditions of the possibility of a particular cognitive system. Language is an essential premise of any cognitive activity because the objects of knowledge are named and both the process and the results are expressed in words, propositions, and images, turning them into specific mediums without which knowledge is impossible.

Through knowledge, man enters different areas of reality in order to possess it; in this sense, philosophic tradition distinguishes four different forms of knowledge: *empiric*, also called vulgar, which is the popular, unmethodical, and unsystematic knowledge, through which the common man knows the facts and their apparent order; *scientific*, through which one methodically transcends the phenomenon, the causes and laws that rule it are known; *philosophical*, comprised of principles that are relative to the essential categories of knowledge that are common to all the sciences; *theological*, referring to the revelation of God, understood as a dogmatic body in which reason is left at the service of faith.

The process of knowledge includes four fundamental elements: *man's cognitive activity, the means of knowledge, the objects of knowledge, and the results of cognitive activity.*

Scientific knowledge involves two dimensions, a *subjective* one, which understands it as a human systematic knowledge that allows understanding reality, a developed skill that dominates knowledge and the relation of its contents; and an *objective* one, understood as a set of logically entwined objective propositions that correspond to the systematic nature of the subjectively comprehended science.[2]

Science is constructed considering the empirical-spontaneous aspect as a condition that is necessary for knowledge.

2 I.M. Bochenski. *Current Methods of Thought*, p. 31

The empirical-spontaneous process of knowledge is susceptible to being accomplished by any human in that it is the possibility to know the objects with which one has contact in practice, where work instruments are means of knowledge of the world:

> The objects of the empirical-spontaneous process of knowledge are first of all instruments and objects of work [...] the historical development of the instruments of work is deeply related to the development of a real knowledge of the surrounding world... within the frames of this process a great amount of world objects have been assimilated and recognized.[3]

This type of knowledge corresponds to the indispensable description of scientific knowledge

Western rationalism, in spite of the differences established by the different philosophical trends, attributes objectivity, systematization, demonstration and logical or empirical ascertainment as essential qualities of scientific knowledge.

Thomas Kuhn believes in the improbability of definite verifications of scientific knowledge, and Popper emphasizes falsifiability as an essential element of scientific knowledge; these criteria discern the anti-dogmatic essence of the scientific task.

Kuhn considers that normal science can be identified with a research based on one or more past scientific realizations that a certain scientific community recognizes in a certain moment as the foundation for its later practice, the study of paradigms is what prepares the student for forming part of a particular scientific community; the successive transition from one paradigm to another by means of a revolution is the usual pattern of development of a mature science.

Popper, on the other hand, understands its objective criticism in the sense of the method of science that consists of rehearsing possible

---

3 J.M. Aróstegui and others. *Scientific Knowledge Methodology*, p. 168

solutions to accessible problems, under the supposition that all criticism is an attempt of rebuttal, and so he proposes a solution rehearsal method submitted into critical control in which there are two fundamental concepts: approximation and explicative power.[4]

The Kuhnian paradigm is understood as a set of beliefs, values, techniques, etc., shared by members of a given community. Scientific revolutions, which are inevitable for the progress of knowledge, result of the rejection of the paradigm and the consequential transformation of the scientific imagination. The assimilation of change requires a reconstruction of the previous theory and an evaluation of the facts.

Kuhn's consideration emphasizes the need for openness in all the sciences and disciplines since rejecting the rigidity and pretension of a definite knowledge encourages the imagination that allows creating new ideologies and executing the accumulative task of renewed scientific knowledge.

In spite of the multiple polemics surrounding the characteristics of scientific knowledge, its consideration as a rational activity that attempts systematic objectivity is undoubtedly agreed upon – its search for coherence; and it is precisely logic, understood as a science of reasoning, what rescues the previous epistemological considerations.

Logic includes, among other disciplines, logic in its strictly formal aspect –according to the laws of association of the concepts that govern the judgments and implications-, intimately linked to methodology.

Methodology constitutes a chapter in epistemology that is relative to the different forms of research. Method comes from the Greek *meta*, "along or throughout", and *ódós*, "path or way"; and so, it literally means "going through the right path, the path of knowledge". Methodology is, consequently, the theory of method, science of the straight thought that guides and arranges knowledge with its own resources for which a microscope and chemical reagents are of no

4 Thomas Kuhn. *Scientific Revolutions Structure*, pp. 33-36 and Karl Popper. *Scientific Researching Logic*, p. 28 and on.

use, where "the only means that is available to us, in this sphere, is the ability of abstraction".[5]

Method, according to what has been observed, literally and etymologically, is the path that leads to knowledge; it expresses the most completed product that logic elaborates and its systematic culmination. In method, the concepts of the theory "turn into other methodical instruments and even entire disciplines are useful [as methods] as frequently occurs in the case of mathematics".[6]

Antonio Alonso considers method, justly, as protector of the objective neutrality of knowledge in all stages of the scientific process.

The formulation of method, according to Eli de Gortari, is obtained through:

a) The deep analysis of the scientific activity, determining its different elements with precision.
b) The systematic study of the relationships that link these elements, both the tested and the potential ones.
c) The ordered and integrated structuring of these elements and their relationships, to rebuild the methodical operations in a higher level and to a greater extent.
d) The generalization of the methodical processes that emerge within a discipline.

Grawitz, on the other hand, proposes four fundamental meanings of the term 'method':

1. Method, in the philosophical sense, is the highest level of abstraction and it designates the logical procedures, which are inherent to any scientific research and, therefore, independent of any specific content.

---

5 Carlos Marx, *The Capital*, p. XIII
6 José Antonio Alonso. *Methodology*, p. 17

2. Method, as a concrete attitude toward the object, which determines the particular manners of organizing the research in a precise and complete manner.
3. Method linked to the efforts of explanation, which supposes a particular philosophical position that affects the stages of research.
4. Method linked to a specific field of knowledge, which implies a particular manner of acting.

In this sense, the list of terminologies provided by Bochenski, related to methodological activity, is pertinent due to its feasibility in affecting design:

1. *Ontological terminology*, referring to the fact that the world is made of *things* like plants, furniture, posters, etc., which are determined by different properties: colour, form, texture, etc., and organized among each other through *relationships.*

   Influenced by Heidegger's philosophy, a generic name is given to all that exists or might be an *entity*, in which two aspects can be distinguished, its *essence*, meaning what the entity is, and its *existence*, consisting of the manner in which it is manifested.

   Thus, the world can be thought of as a group of *configurations* of entities that are considered in their manifestations, that is, in their existence and in their possibility of being.

2. *Gnoseological terminology*, referring to the true or false quality that is attributable to any proposition, this way, -without getting into the question of truth – a proposition is considered true if something corresponds to it, that is, an entity that exists, and on the contrary false if its content alludes to something that does not exist.

   Every science tends to build true principles as a last finality of scientific knowledge that may be accomplished in two ways: by apprehending the configuration sensibly or intellectually: to know if the clause "*this table is dark*" is true, suffice it to look at the table. This knowledge is called *direct.* The second is obtained by inferring the configuration in regards to other contents. This is the *indirect* knowledge. Any interpretation based on signs is indirect knowledge.

3. *Psychological terminology*, referring to the subjective conditions of knowledge, that is, as a psychic phenomenon, limited to human knowledge as a property, in that any knowledge is the knowledge of a particular person.

   Knowledge always has an object: what is known. This object is always a configuration. What is known is always a thing or a property, content. This way, the object becomes knowledge. Things, properties and relations transform into concepts; the contents, into propositions.

   These images may be considered in their subjective aspect as psychic or mental products; or in their objective aspect in regards to the content, that is, to what they represent. This way, it is necessary to distinguish between the concept and the subjective propositions that are relative to it and the concept and the objective propositions that define it.

   Knowledge is the result of the subject's cognitive activity: to know, and it ends with the judgment that affirms or denies a proposition.

   It is necessary to distinguish between knowing and thinking. Thinking is the psychic movement that leads from one object to another, knowing is the result of a certain way of thinking.

4. *Semeiotic terminology*, referring to the fact that in order to communicate concepts and propositions or to facilitate thought, symbols are used, preferentially of the written or oral language that consists of words or equivalent symbols.

   Language represents concepts and propositions.

   "Name" is the symbol of an objective concept and "statement" is the symbol of an objective proposition.

These are general considerations that affect the methodology and which, due to the historical nature of knowledge, must be completed with the information that each field of knowledge generates, to obtain an "adequate methodology to achieve its objective and to make use of the most conductive techniques".[7] This way, science structures the knowledge acquired and employs logical elements combined with scientific imagination.

The structural rigor is not exclusive to a certain area of knowledge. The basic languages of communication - Taylor affirms -, including music, dance, or mathematics, are based on highly formalized rules and disciplines whose pattern did not condition their development. The human being has always lived under norms and patterns that socially discipline him, hence the general methodology whose constants are applicable to any particular methodology.

All scientific conceptions are structured based on a tripartite system whose outline consists of theory, method and technique. In the domain of methodology, "the philosophical activity consists of elaborating the theories of the different methods used in scientific research, understanding their foundation, their general laws, etc".[8]

The role of technique is to provide the manual operations that are most suitable for the principles of the theory and the method. Every technique is a practical procedure:

> [...] a set of rules capable of efficiently running any activity and having the dexterity to carry it out [...] a procedure or set of procedures that are demanded for the use of an instrument, for the use of a material, or for the handling of a certain situation within a process.[9]

Method, as an abstract conceptual process, lacks sense if not expressed through a language and applied in a practical manner for the

[7] Eli de Gortari. *General Methodology and Special Methods*, p. 12

[8] J. A. Alonso. *Op. cit.*, p. 11

[9] Eli de Gortari, *Op. cit.*, p. 16

transformation of reality. Consequently, it is evident that theory, method and technique form the elements of any scientific practice and should be comprehended by their mutual relationships and not independent from one another.

Knowledge remains, and through it certain practical activities are performed, in which the knowledge is used repeatedly and always as an organized set of mental operations.

In the formulation of a method, the theoretic conditions of a research are correlated, which are understood as general characters of the method "that are extracted by the logic of the scientific activity, and are later itemized in each of the disciplines [...] arranged according to the specific peculiarities of the processes studied in them".[10]

The diversity of study subjects and the differences that result of the different philosophical trends have created numerous classifications of methods, among them and in a primordially illustrative manner, those that stand out due to their determinant factors are:

a) *Historical*, which projects the correspondence between the logical research expressed in the different methods and the scientific theories that have revolutionized the ideologies of the world; thus, Eli de Gortari exemplifies: the application of Aristotle's deductive logic is consummated in Euclid's geometry; Bacon exposes for the first time within the philosophical field and in a systematic and explicit manner the inductive aspect: to generalize starting from links observed between the particular facts; and it is Galileo who develops the theory and practice of induction in Physics.

   This author emphasizes the existing relationship between Hegel's dialectics and the method employed by Marx to establish the periodicity of history based on economic development. In fact, Marx takes from Hegel the structure of the process of thought: dialectics as a fundamental structure of the universe, even

---

[10] Ibid, p. 18

though it does not completely follow the principles from which it is developed: my dialectic method, writes Marx is not only different from the Hegelian, but is its direct opposite. To Hegel, the life-process of the human brain, i.e. the process of thinking, which, under the name of 'the idea', he even transforms into an independent subject, is the demiurge of the real world.

With me, on the contrary, the ideal is nothing else than the material world reflected by the human mind [...] with him (Hegel) it is standing on its head. It must be turned right side up again, if you would discover the rational kernel within the mystical shell.[11]

b) *Technological*, which is based on the idea that social development is basically determined by technological changes invented, developed or adopted by the societies.
c) *Economic*, which sustains the preeminence of economic and commercial powers that act after the technological innovations. According to this interpretation, the technologies developed and chosen at a certain time and place are the most adequate for the existing economic conditions.
d) *Political*, based on the thesis that, in spite of technological and economic imperatives, the dominating political powers are the ones that determine the social organization and research development.
e) *Ideological*, which sustains that the election or proposition of methods lies in the predominant ideals, beliefs, and values as a whole, which constitute the '*image of the world*' or dominant ideology of a given society.[12]

Clarifying that the previous are only some of the factors that determine the methodological characteristics and their influence on the results of research, and that their incidence field is different in a way that some of them specially affect the dominion of social sciences, out of

---

11 Carlos Marx, *Op. cit.*, pgs. XXIII-XXIV

12 Nigel Cross and others, *Designing the Future.*

the different classifications of methodology, we take from Bochenski the distinction of two types of methods:

1. The method of practical thought, which refers to something that can be done by the thinker, which is employed when a knowledge is sought, but a knowledge of how, that is, how can this or that be done.
2. The method of theoretic thought, which refers to the contents that may be learned independently of their practical use.

We can also distinguish:

3. The Method of direct knowledge. A phenomenological method understood as a method of the intellectual intuition and of the description of the intuited.
4. The method of indirect knowledge, already mentioned, which includes linguistic analysis, deduction and reduction.[13]

All these methods have in common the methods of fundamental reasoning, derived from logic:

Deductive method or deduction, which is the classical method of a priori reasoning according to which particular cases are derived from general concepts or, in other words, concepts are derived from the facts.

Inductive method or induction, a classical form of reasoning of physical sciences attributed to Bacon, characterized by establishing the concepts based on the facts, reasoning from the general to the particular, and unlike deduction, which establishes necessary truths, it arrives at probable truths.

The partial nature of the previous characterizations and their confusion between theory, method and technique is made obvious.

---

[13] I.M. Bochenski, *Op. cit.*, pgs. 92-41

It is a fact that in the different fields of knowledge, theories, methods and techniques are applied, which as a whole form a research strategy made suitable for the scientific demands of each case, to obtain the best results and, in the case of design, to conduct modifications of the reality that is purported: architectonic, industrial or graphic.

Thus, the logical formulation of research methods in each discipline requires a previous analysis of the nature of the activities of that discipline in order to determine them plainly.

Scientific activity evolves, conditioned by a constant confrontation with unknown situations, of which there is no precise knowledge nor definite formulas, the problems "can be theoretical or practical, abstract or concrete [...] they involve the need to find the answer to an inquired situation [...] to discover an unknown process, to build objectives, to formulate new concepts".[14]

A method based on theory must precede the raising of problem solving procedures, but the method cannot be the only one or the definite one, the complexity of nature phenomena and society demands the diversification of methods, none of which have absolute value. If they were considered as such, one would fall into what Tomas Maldonado defines as "fetishism of the methods".[15]

One always runs the risk of falling into the trap of believing that theories are universal and ahistorical, and that social sciences only deserve this name if they imitate natural sciences; thus "the preeminence that is given to the quantitative or mathematical techniques (methods according to their nomenclature) is born out of the concern for exact data [...] ignoring typically sociological aspects",[16] as observed in North American positivism.

It is therefore convenient to stress the need to avoid this false scientific rigor and the dogmatic cult to any trend of thought, it is essential

---

[14] Eli de Gortari, *Op. cit.*, pp. 13-14

[15] Tomás Maldonado. *Vanguard and Rationality*, p. 126

[16] J.A. Alonso, *Op. cit.*, pgs.13-14

for scientific attitude to have a critical nature that allows knowledge openness that is necessary for its development without limiting the established methods.

Design making must formulate methodologies based on the knowledge that science must contribute to its rational support without falling into "the stigma of academic respectability that science enjoys [...] methodology has turned into a ritual and science into a totem".[17]

In view of the variety of methods and methodologies and the frequently sterile disputes derived from the different scientific trends, Asimow's reflection regarding the need for a philosophy of the researcher in the same way that we have philosophy of history or philosophy of science is not idle, because it is a fact that the complete process of research, regardless of the topic, includes the subject by necessity.

---

[17] Gui Bonsiepe. *Industrial Design Theory and Practice*, p. 146

RESEARCH

A research is a systematized search in which reason and thought analyze in depth the vestiges that explain a phenomenon or a specific object. Research is always manifested as one or several spirals because it constantly returns to the basic concept in order to develop itself and reach a synthesis. Thus, research intervenes in reality through reason and intelligence, transforming knowledge resources into benefits for humanity.

Research or investigate comes from the Latin *vestige, remains, trace*, consequently meaning to follow or search for vestiges, traces of something. In English the word *research* is used and in French *rechercher*, both cases meaning 'to search again'. And so, by research we understand "a cognitive activity of analysis and reflection that is developed in practice, on a practical and real problem, and preceding a particular intervention of reality".[18]

In general, we can say that

> [...] research is a reflective, systematic, controlled and critical process that allows discovering new facts and data, relations or laws, in any field of human knowledge [...] it constitutes a path to knowing reality, to discovering partial truths.[19]

These definitions that are extended or reduced depending on the author, coincide in their essential aspects: research is a formal-systematic process, it includes a structure that involves a summary of procedures and a report of results, it is a specialized study; it is a process that is reflective, rational, critical, controlled, limited, diligent, disciplined, analytical, etc.

However, it is necessary to determine research's relationship with reality.

If we consider Marx's affirmation that "the philosophers have only interpreted the world in various ways; the point is to change it",[20] and the review published in *The European Messenger*, dedicated to the method of *The Capital*, stating that "not the idea, but the material phenomenon alone can serve as a starting point. Such an inquiry will confine itself to the confrontation and the comparison of a fact, not with ideas, but with another fact",[21] we can conclude that research is the link

---

18 Gian A. Gilli. *How to Research*, p. 8

19 Ezequiel Ander-Egg. "Introduction to Researching Techniques" in *Social Sciences Methodology*, p. 37

20 Carlos Marx, *Feuerbach Thesis and other Phylosophical Writings*, p. 12

21 Carlos Marx. *The Capital*, p. 91

that establishes a base for man's activity aimed at the transformation of reality.

In regards to this subject, Marx himself distinguishes the mode of exposition from the mode of research, "research has to appropriate the material in detail, to analyze its different forms of development and to track down their inner connection. Only after this work has been done, can the real movement be appropriately presented",[22] this way specifying the role of research as a form of understanding reality.

Selltiz affirms that research always begins with a question or a specific problem of various natures; it starts with the observation of a fact or a series of facts and continues with the search for an explanation of its conditions of possibility.

There are two types of reasons to ask questions that lead to research: *intellectual*, based on the desire to understand the facts and *practical*, based on the desire to know in order to do.

Based on this, the resulting research can be pure or applied, while the research of practical problems can lead to discovering basic principles and basic research often leads to practical use.

Research defined as a logical answer to a specific question presents different degrees of complexity: *description, explanation and prediction,* although *description* is considered a preparatory stage.

Classification consists of defining the relationships between the varieties of phenomena categories.

Explanation consists of the conceptual determination of phenomena.

Umberto Eco, on the other hand, states that:

> Research discusses a recognizable and defined object in a way so as to make it recognizable to others [...] an 'object'

---

22 *Ibid.*, p. XXIII

> that has the possibility of being an object of scientific inquiry [...] a susceptible object of discourse.

A research says things that have not yet been said about an object, or it reviews from a different view than things that have been said. Research has to be useful for others. These would be, in general terms, the fundamental requisites for a research that purports to be scientific.[23]

Man's cognitive activity, in addition to the sensible and conceptual representations that it provides, plays a role in practical action with things; "practical activity is related to the use of work instruments and the material means of knowledge, with the transformation of some objects with the help of others".[24]

Research is precisely the practical action and it is considered one of two main characteristics of scientific practice; according to Alonso, these two components are research and theory, and their relation is: theory is the 'set of concepts', definitions, and propositions interrelated among each other, which present us with a systematic vision of the phenomena by identifying the relation among the variables, with the objective of explaining and predicting these same phenomena

> [...] scientific research, on the other hand, can be defined as the systematic, controlled, empirical and critical search for the hypothetical propositions regarding the relations among phenomena.[25]

It can be affirmed that research is the backbone of scientific practice because in its development it conjugates theory –as the set of means and instruments of intellectual work -, method – as an abstraction of the coherence of concrete knowledge -, and technique – understood as *praxis*, a transformation of reality-.

---

23 Umberto Eco. *How to do a Thesis*, pp. 49-50

24 J.M. Aróstegui, *Op. cit.*, p. 159

25 J.A. Alonso, *Op. cit.*, p. 25

All the elements of scientific practice are susceptible to isolated explanation; in reality, however, they cannot be apart; both man's subjective activity and the objective practice form a single attitude of the individual faced with the world's phenomena.

The importance of this conjunction is made evident in social practice, because in the manner in which objects of knowledge are being appropriated, these are no longer conceived under "the form of contemplation" –says Marx-, but from the praxis viewpoint, which captures each phenomenon as an element of the whole, inscribed in reality.

Scientific research is established, then, as an inseparable and unifying element of all methodological theses, because it is practiced in all the fields of knowledge with direct link to general methodology,

> [...] the differences are specific [...] they are produced with the particularization of method [...] according to the specific sphere and to the objective characteristics of the processes involved [...] the method is particularized in as many fields as there are scientific disciplines.[26]

Consequently, every method includes research, which includes its own methodological and technical conditions that are not confused with the particular methodologies.

Technique is understood as a set of "rigorous operative procedures that are well-defined, transmissible and susceptible to being applied repeatedly under the same conditions; choosing a technique depends on the sought objective and the method of development".[27]

Research techniques are the resources of intellectual work conditioned by the method.

It is indispensable to respect the coherence of the chosen techniques with the method and to respect the degree of complexity of the

---

[26] Carlos Marx. *Op. cit.*, p. 9

[27] Eli de Gortari, *Op. cit.*, p. 45

concepts in relation to which these techniques are employed, because the appropriate relation between thought and reality depends on it.

Scientific research demands manual and intellectual practices and skills, "it should be conducted with intelligence, imagination and patience, under the highest rational rigor and the strictest objectivity",[28] considering that it is in practice where man has to prove the truth.

Language is inherent to research techniques, because it is the vehicle of thought and man's cognitive faculty transcends through it.

It is evident that the selection of research techniques cannot be arbitrary or intuitive; it rather corresponds to the theoretical and methodological fundaments of research.

Research tools are similar for all disciplines, nevertheless, just like techniques, they cannot be identical in all aspects; their selection and employment, although corresponding to general principles, have to be adapted to their particular applications.

Research techniques form part of the intellectual artistry, which demands discipline and order as ineludible conditions and includes taking notes, forming files, etc.

The importance of research in design methodology has been widely notable, for example, Ricard says that a previous phase, [...] which is a must in all creative act, is that in which basic data are assimilated, this preliminary inquiry facilitates the necessary data [...] regarding the essence, behaviour and possibilities of all that is somehow implicated in that operative area.[29]

On the other hand, Christopher Alexander reaffirms in his *Notes on the Synthesis of Form* that design is the research process of physical things that exhibit a new physical order, an organization, and new forms, in response to the function.

---

28 *Idem.*

29 André Ricard. *Design Why?*, p. 122

Indeed, in order to know an object, it is necessary to study all its aspects, all its relations, this is a demand for universality, and even though one does not manage to know the object in its totality, the researcher must do everything possible to accomplish a complete objective determination.

The will to know is intimately related to the will to survive, and both provide humans with a constant diachronic labour of problem solving, thus [...] man has engaged in the task of solving problems [...] a phenomenon that perhaps can be expressed in terms of 'hominization', meaning, a phylogenetic process that made possible the emergence and consolidation of man as a species [...] surviving as a problem solver.[30]

Design is a highly problematic discipline; to begin with, Selle says, because it plays a determining role in the implementation or reinforcement of an agreement regarding the interpretation and transformation of reality.

When the designer formulates the problem of design, as in any scientific discipline, he must also be a researcher: in order to study whether the problem has a solution, he must know what demands must be fulfilled, because the contemporary, highly technical world requires knowing the results of knowledge, which are indispensable for the creation of better projects.

Every creative act requires enough knowledge to comprehend its consequences. That is why the designer must fulfil the demands of the scientific task: *a sense of observation, a taste for precision, imagination, curiosity, impartiality, and all the attitudes required for objectivity*.

Even when the process of creation is tied to formulas, there is a need for research, as it provides the designer with the possibility to foresee different interpretations according to the objective and subjective elements that may be involved.

---

[30] T. Maldonado, *Op. cit.*, p. 125

DESIGN METHODOLOGY

All designs, as autonomous disciplines, have their own methodologies that derive from the general methodology. The theories can be intradisciplinary, multidisciplinary, and interdisciplinary, and the results of their possible relationships are the theoretical perspectives expressed in a model to design, or to understand what is already designed. In the examples, diagrams display the operating methods of diaphragm aperture, the nominative description of a bicycle, the morphological and chromatic model of a Theo Van Doesburg painting from 1920 and Barry Boehm's spiral development model from 1985, used today in software engineering.

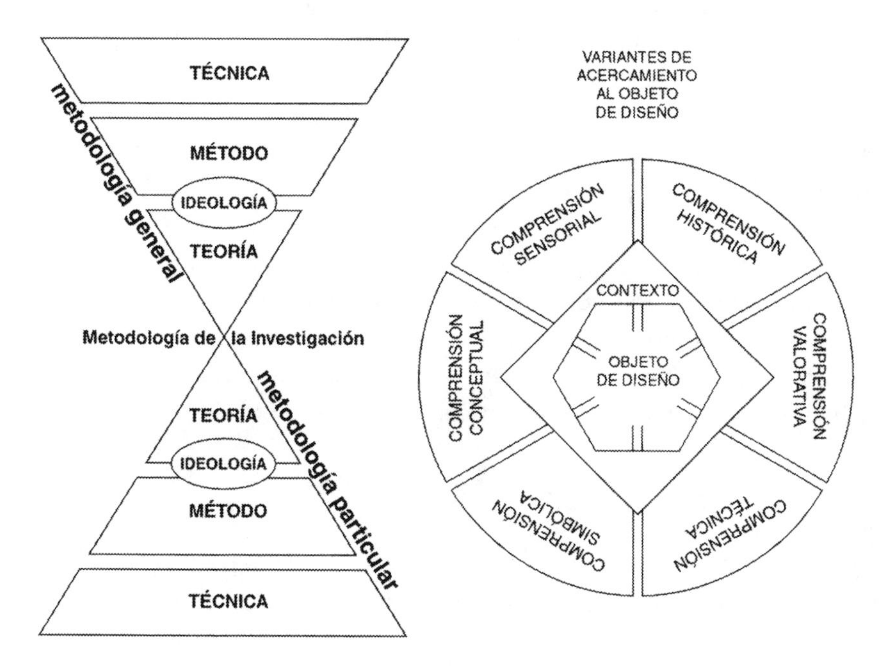

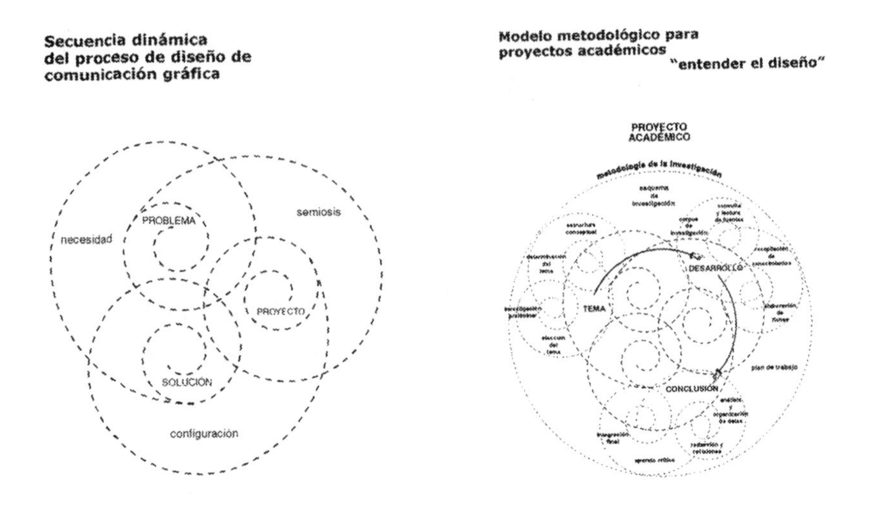

In a wide sense and taking the meaning of words to the extreme, there are some who, inspired by professional eagerness, consider that all men are designers if design is understood as 'any conscious effort to establish a significant order', and in a similar sense, it is also affirmed that man has always designed even if throughout history the manner in which he has done it has changed.

The fact is that man transforms his environment. Surely, man's needs were what drove him to develop his first cultural manifestations that transformed his relationship with nature as a consequence of his *process* of alloplastic *adaptation*, related to the *changing of the environment*, which differs from the autoplastic kind, which consists of the *mere adaptation of the organism*.

It is worth mentioning that added to the basic needs for food, clothes, residence, etc. are the needs for cultural development products that are associated with the first needs and modified, and so, for example, the need to quench thirst is combined with the need to do so with a specific recipient, and furthermore with a selected beverage.

It is reasonable to suppose that the first cultural manifestations are located within the fields of agriculture and handicrafts, in the production of sowing artifacts and objects for eating, and that these were the result of intuition given by reflection.

Handmade work is characterized by the control that its author has on the totality of the design cycle: from the moment of the object's conception to its production, and so the manufacturing process can be improved or perfected; the author has the tools for its production, he is in direct contact with the reality in which the object fulfils its specific goal, he works according to his own lineaments and arranges the object at his own will; he knows what the recipient's needs are.

The crafting process is perfected through a trial-and-error relationship that allows for a continuous process of selection that is still used in our days and thanks to which many crafts are used in the same way and conserve the same form as thousands of years ago.

If we thoroughly examine handmade products, we can find subtle forms suggestive of the deepest complexity, which are so much more surprising if we keep in mind that they are products of a non-deliberate effort of design. The explanation of this phenomenon can be found in the gradual adjustment of objects with their finality, which little by little creates an adequate form according to their operation. Justly, Löbach affirms that before industrial production, artisans had an enormous range of freedom to introduce variants and include emotional figuration without boundaries.

During handicraft production, the operative, manoeuvre and elaboration stages are inseparable, but starting from the 17th century, the scientific spirit of the Renaissance contributes science's rigor to technological progress and the segregation of these aspects begins. However, B. Löbach indicates that in the mid 19th century objects for use were still manufactured mainly manually, differentiating two types of manual productions:

1. *Products mainly marked by their practical function* and which were often named after functional forms, such as tableware.
2. *Handcrafted products whose importance is mainly symbolic;* even though they may have practical functions, they are mainly used as representative objects of the social ***status***, for instance, jewellery and textiles.

The nature of craft production carries a series of obstacles for its evolution, among these obstacles, the following are worth mentioning:

- Original designs are anonymous and become lost in time.
- The designs' modifications frequently result from errors in the transmission of techniques.
- Knowledge regarding the designs' development is basically passed through the objects themselves.

With the economic transformations and the arrival of industrial production, the artisan loses control of the product of his work and, consequently, of the design process; the emerging society slowly separates him from the recipient and the production machine generates the specialization. Nevertheless, this same process turns design into a conscious process, a phenomenon that initiates the acknowledgement and cultivation of individuality in design.

The creative discipline that today we call design emerges as a consequence of the new circumstances that the Industrial Revolution imposes on the creative process, obliging its differentiation from mere production.

The industrial process alters the *creation-elaboration-distribution* process, which is characteristic of the handicraft process, and which makes possible unexpected adjustments, because the industry demands functional safety in all stages of production: exactly what is foreseen is reproduced.

In this regards, the most important consequence of the new industrial era is the loss of source of motivation for giving way to a new form of creation as an abstract action, not emerging directly from the contact with reality, the creative vain can no longer flow from that palpable reality, but from am hypothetical plausible reality.

> The future users are no longer known people, but an abstract and anonymous element called 'the public' to which a supposed standardized behaviour is attributed [...] it is no

> longer possible to have a feed-back with reality, nor to have an intuitive understanding of that reality.[31]

Due to these evident transformations, contemporary authors have established the different stages of the evolution of design, this way Jordi Llovet distinguishes: the *naturalistic stage,* or the one corresponding to primitive societies; the *intermediate inventive stage,* prior to the emergence of industrial bourgeois society, and *consumer stage,* corresponding to the industrialized society determined by the market's demands.

In the first stage, there were no useless objects, all the created objects obeyed a need and were an adequate and possible solution. Their basic purpose is efficiency; their utility in economic terms is exclusively the value of their use.

In the inventive stage, objects are created from memory and reflection, in a manner similar to similar situations. During the first period, the designer must discover, in the second, the designer reflects on the invention of solutions that are adequate to the historical circumstances; for the reflection, relationships with previous objects are combined in order to create new ones.

In this stage, the invention of objects is determinant for the acceleration of the process of civilization, and during this stage, due to abundance, the first completely useless artifacts appear.

In economical terms, the objects acquire, in addition to a useful value, a symbolic value, because each culture characterizes its own objects and endows them with a particular meaning.

The third stage is characterized by the incorporation of a value of change to the object, because the production determined by the sales-consumption relation conditions the design. Evidently, the natural and cultural elements continue to be factors of the design.

---

[31] A. Ricard, *Op. cit.*, pp. 186-187

Rupert de Ventós names *implicated art* the evolutionary continuity of design that does not attempt to explain the world but becomes involved in it, it does not attempt to "inform about it as much as to form part of it, represent it as much as resolve it, recreate it as much as reform it [...] it does not seek perfect forms but relevant and articulate forms".[32]

In this last stage, design demands to be shaped in a different manner through the analysis of the factors that determine the form, in order to conciliate them in such as way that the intuitive and schematic methods are insufficient, doomed to fail.

Design is called *designi* in Italian, *dessin* in French and *diseño* in Spanish, and in all of these cases it is the verbal name of the corresponding verb that comes from the Italian *disegnare* which comes from the Latin *designare*: to mark, to designate.

In its broadest meaning, design is an activity performed in social systems of institutions and so it involves some knowledge regarding the needs that are generated in them. Design is a working tool, an integrating activity, a science of encounter, humanism, an operative means.

Design is, therefore, a discipline directed toward the solving of problems that man raises in his continuous process of adaptation, according to his physical and spiritual needs.

Designing consists of projecting the environment where man lives in order to establish a meaningful order; this is why it is a fundamental task manifested in nearly all our conscious activities, which require a formal and expressive definition.

Although the essential task of the designer consists of transforming the environment, which is expressed in objects that in the broad sense modify man himself, there is no consensus regarding the conditions of

---

32 Xavier Rupert de Ventós. "Applied Art – Involved Art" in J. S. de Antuñano (comp.) *Design Process*, p. 17

this process. Design is a quotidian language of which we still do not know how to report.

Designing is the object of study activity of design, which as a discipline studies the behaviour of the forms, their combinations, their associative coherence, their practical possibilities and the aesthetic values that are captured in their integrity. The integrating factor of this process is constituted by the *interaction of the design, the designer and the designed.*

Design is identified with the task, the human action whose characterization must satisfy, among other determinations, the following:

Being a movement or a conscious change originating in the agent himself; it is a *praxis* that can be *immanent*, if it wears out in the agent himself, like thinking, or *transcendent*, if it concludes outside the agent, like writing or designing.

According to Aristotelian tradition, the *praxis* that is accomplished in the result of the action, that is the transcendent type, is *poiesis.*

Poiesis can be: *creative*, when adding to the being something that did not exist before, to which art corresponds par excellence; *reiterative*, if it only produces what already exists according to already established features and the products turn out similar.

This way design can be characterized as a specific form of art, like a *poetic praxis*, and as such responds to a particular function, which may be of communication, comfort, organization, recreation, etc.

That which is designed comprises the result of the action, whose variety includes everything from houses, furniture, instruments, machines, signage systems, books, magazines, newspapers, posting signs, stamps, animation drawings, pamphlets, front pages, etc.

It is important to point out the impact of design on semeiotics, because this explains the need to satisfy the demands of rationality according to which symbols constitute a way of transforming things, in order to create realities that lead to other realities.

Giving a meaning to things determines our attitude and our behaviour: when a rock is carved, it is being designed and turned into a knife or a mortar hand, which at the same time means hunting or food and, in both cases, human behaviours.

The designer articulates and organizes the elements of the design so that man can understand, assimilate and use them, and in that sense he is a specialist who must establish a relation between the object's morphology and the goals of the recipients, and he must not be alien to the operative problems at stake; he is not a technologist nor an inventor, but the tasks that his activity must fulfil demand creative imagination and mastery of the techniques.

Due to the diversity of the goals of design, their classifications are as varied as they are pointless, because they depend on current social relations and historic cultural determinations. And so the classifications turn out as exemplificative, like Jordi Llovet, who distinguishes: industrial design, graphic design, urban design and environmental design; or Löbach, who refers to specialties such as: regional and territorial planning, landscape planning and configuration, and urban planning and configuration, which are affected by architecture, industrial design and the configuration of means of communication.

Munari, from the designer's point of view, classifies design into: *visual,* concerning communicative images: signs, signals, symbols, meaning of shapes and colours, etc.; *industrial,* related to the design of objects for use and the study of means and materials; *graphic,* related to the world of imprint, printed books, etc. and *research,* dedicated to experimenting with structures and the choices of materials' combination.

Morris Asimow adds engineering design as that which is determined by highly sophisticated technological factors.

It is worth mentioning *styling*, an ephemeral and superficial design focused exclusively on external appearance and linked to fashion, with no responsibility whatsoever for the content and quality of the form, reason why it is justly considered a 'parody of design' because if it were to be considered design in the strict sense, it would be necessary to redefine design both as an object of study and as a discipline because, to say it in Bonsiepe's words, it makes the concept of form seem suspicious.

Cultural development involves the construction and transformation of objects created by man, and so it is convenient to separate and organize the knowledge of the objects with which man relates in order to distinguish the practices that are possible with these objects; thence the historical need to formulate particular methodologies, among them, design.

The expression 'design methodology', as design itself, includes an extensive sphere, a set of disciplines in which the fundamental aspect is the conception and development of projects that allow us to foresee how things should be and to think up the tools suitable for the pre-established objectives.

Consequently, design methodology integrates sets of indications and prescriptions for solving the problems of design; it determines the most adequate sequence of actions, their content, and the specific procedures.

Methodological propositions have no goals per se, they conserve the nature of the intellectual instruments of the general methodology; therefore, they should not be confused –as happens frequently –; design methods are recipes or strict routines whose application, if followed scrupulously, guarantees optimum goals, they include technical knowledge that should be adapted according to the specific circumstances and goals.

Method can neither be understood as one and only, universal, valid for any type of research or problem; methods – in plural – always refer to particularities and provide partial solutions, and so it is more appropriate to refer to design methodology as the study of the structure of the design process.

Methodological design is a systematic form of thought that results of the theoretic articulation of the analytical discourses in which the discipline is immersed; thence it is a phenomenological synthesis of the design process.

The idea of incorporating into the practice of design scientific disciplines has been encouraged since beginning of the century, among others, by architect Lethaby and by Hannes Meyer from Bauhaus at the end of the 1920's, who tried to link figurative principles and design processes to scientific-theoretic principles; subsequently, the Ulm School of Design founded its project with the temptation to integrate science to design, this occurred in a time when other schools were still in the pre-scientific stage of design based on emotional figurative procedures. Consequently, the idea emerged that design requires help from science.

However, in this regard, Selle observes that the methods and procedures that are currently available to designers are rather due to economic pressures that force the rationalization of the processes, both for the market as for advertising. The consequence is that the last decades have suffered from a growing '*methodolatry*' and that the propositions of models for knowing, recompiling, arranging, comparing, projecting, etc. are numerous and many of them have no conceptual fundament that is theoretically appropriate for the proposed methods.

The design method should be based on logical structures that have given proof of their aptitude and must go hand in hand with creative capabilities. Exercising the intellect is not contrary to the expressive intention nor to the creative capacity; on the contrary, they complement each other.

Systematization is useful in the field of design to avoid arbitrary and incoherent actions in the intuitive paths through the vast range of possibilities presented in each project.

Method, in design, is determined by the goals: it responds to specific problems, and so being familiar with the methods is not enough, it is necessary to know how to apply them to the given situations.

Several theoreticians agree on four methodological constants in design:

1. *Information and research*: consisting of gathering and arranging the material that is relative to the particular case or problem.

2. *Analysis:* decomposition of the contextual system into demands, requirements or determinants
3. *Synthesis:* consisting of the proposal of valid criteria for most of the demands and that the whole be manifested as a structured and coherent whole called formal answer to the problem.
4. *Evaluation:* concerning the subsistence of the formal answer in contrast with reality.

To these we can add the formulation of alternatives and the project definition.

These constants in design form the design process, which is produced through a succession of moments of both a '*transparent box*' as well as a '*black box*' [...] in which the behaviour is conceptualizable and momentarily becomes radically imaginative [...] as H. Read points out in *Image and Idea*, "made of mnemonic and eidetic images of information registered by the memory or of associations that are non-translatable into discursive terms".[33]

The designer must keep in mind that inspiration is the work of disciplined thought that must not be confused with regulated thought or stereotyped attitude. The problem's analysis is necessarily the starting point, through which the interrelation between the parts that compose the problem that is to be solved is comprehended, and so its solution depends on it.

The designer must have a method that allows him to perform his project with the adequate material, the necessary techniques, and the form that corresponds to their performance. Finally, the designer must keep in mind that the models can respond to scientific conceptions that may offer the correct solutions but might result in negative social effects. Design is not alien to the contradictions that are given in society nor is it exempt from its ideological consequences.

---

[33] Oscar Olea y Carlos González Lobo. *Analysis and Logic Design*, pp. 15-26

METHODOLOGICAL CONSTANTS

Problem - Project - Solution

Design problems are presented when objects in the surroundings do not help man in his social development, either when culture changes and modifies the manner of doing things, or when a new activity is created. The ability to solve problems is an inherent characteristic of human beings, and problems are solved through knowledge and experience. The designer's primary task is to solve formal problems of aesthetic and functional nature, his answers are always relevant ad his solutions tend to create other problems.

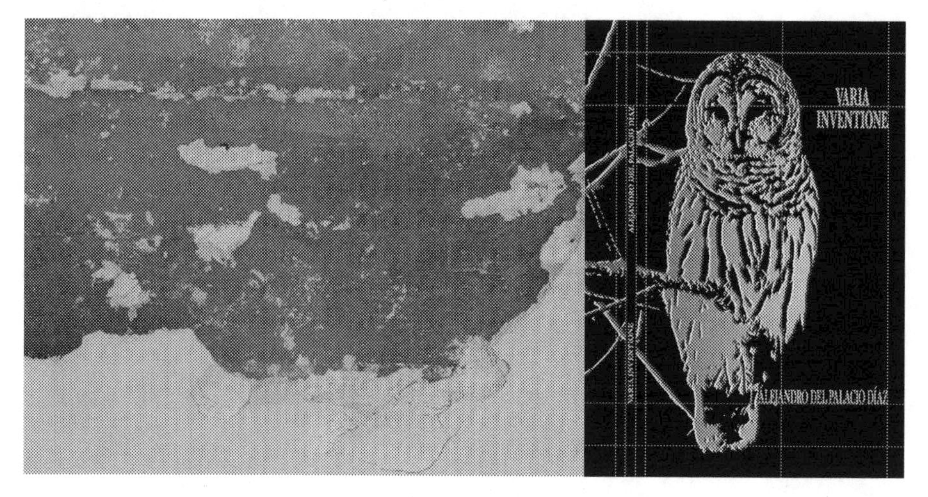

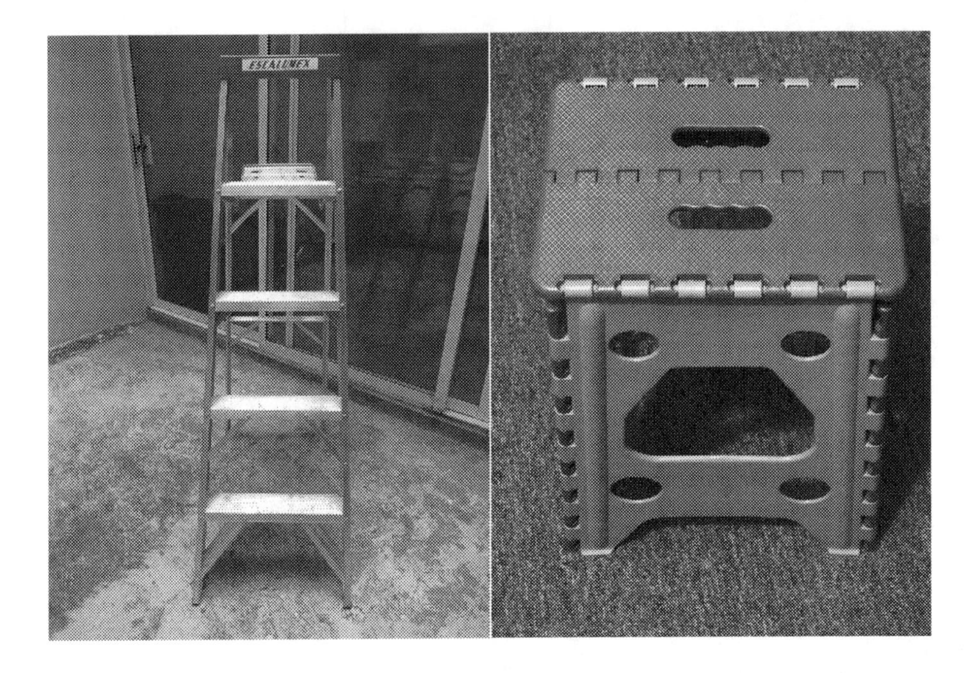

One of the distinctive characteristics of human beings is their capacity to solve problems, but most importantly their capacity to raise them.

By problem we understand "any difficulty that cannot be automatically solved [...] with the sole action of our instinctive reflexes [...] or through the memory of what we have previously learned".[34] Problems are the result of the acting of thought, they are always related and their solutions tend to create other problems.

The ability to solve problems is an inherent feature of the human being, and so the producers of the objects that surround us are not unfamiliar with it. The designer's main task, as several authors agree, consists of solving formal problems of aesthetic and functional nature.

However, the designer's activity does not only consist of solving problems, he also discovers and creates them. Often, the designer identifies problems where nobody images them to exist, this is essential in the creative aspect.

34 Eli de Gortari, Op. cit., p. 39

Every design problem begins "with an effort to accomplish an adjustment between the form in question and its context. The form is the problem's solution; the context defines the problem".[35] Thus, design as an action is guided toward solving conditioned problems that do not necessarily have a sole correct answer: generally, there would be a number of varied answers whose relative exactitude depends on the meaning that is given to the data sorting.

The amount of knowledge that is available to the designer for raising a particular problem determines the variety of solutions in such a way that increased knowledge reduces the possibilities of forming new and unexpected forms; only when the designer faces exceptional situations does he apply new basic methods.

Problems in design arise when the objects surrounding man do not help him in this social development, either when culture changes and modifies the way in which things are conducted or when a new activity is created. In spite of the vagueness of this consideration, we can mention, without pretending to be thorough, the group of sectors in which the problems of design are located:

- *Ornamental decoration*: maximum utilization of the living space, functional lighting of environments, acoustics, circulation of air and odours, hygiene services, correct use of textures and colours, heating and refrigeration, fabrics, tapestry, etc. in offices, public localities, hospitals, homes, schools, restaurants, entertainment spaces and others.
- *Clothing industry*: clothes for daily use, work clothes, sports, footwear and special security equipment, etc.
- *Measuring instruments*: thermometers, scales, barometers, seismographs, etc.
- *Educational games*: outdoors, school, the beach, the water, air, thermal, optical, dynamic, can be dismantled and convertible, useful or artistic, etc.

---

[35] Christopher Alexander. *Form Synthesis Essay*, p. 21

- *Museography*: special structures, technical exhibitions, temporary demountable structures, lighting, ambiance, signposting, tour study, presentation of models and reproductions, etc.
- *Recreation areas*: transportation, facilities, space, communication with the public, etc.
- *Gardens*: decorative objects' design and arrangement, lighting, kiosks, fountains, greenhouses, irrigation systems, etc.
- *Old age and disability*: prosthesis, cosmetic surgery, transportation, apparatuses and instruments, etc.
- *Advertising*: fixed or mobile, internal or external, small or large format, etc.
- *Facilities and graphics in fairs and exhibitions*: fair compounds, placards, signposting, symbols, prints, etc.
- *Page make-up*: publications: bulletin, magazine, newspaper, seminar, web pages, etc.
- *Signposting*: public, interior, vial, architectonic, etc.
- *Film and TV*: titles, effects, texts, animation, editing, etc.
- *Graphic arts*: serigraphy, print types: xerography, batik, monotype, etc.
- *Textile industry*: textures, colours, tapestry, etc.
- *Department stores*: identity, installation, counters, shelving, signposting, points of sale, merchandise exhibition, etc.
- *Travelling items*: suitcases, bags, trucks, etc.
- *Graphics on architecture*: store signs, department stores, illuminated advertising signboards, factory brands, symbols, distant signs, etc.
- *Packaging, wrapping and boxing*: labelling, containers, transportation, collocation, materials, etc.
- *Editorial activity*: format, paper, colour/ink, colour/paper, bookbinding, typography, illustrations, photographs, in bulletins, posters, newspapers, magazines, books, e-books, etc.

In fact, the complexity of design and of its applications impedes the accurate definition of its own sphere and makes its multidisciplinary nature obvious; what can be defined, as has been done, are its formal and material contents.

It must be clarified that the solution for design problems requires study and research, and the ability to know how to raise the problems in a way that they are individualized and without confusion, thus defining the means that they require, because a problem whose raising is not linked to the specific study of its possibilities of solution is actually a pseudo-problem.

However, solutions to design problems are not a direct consequence of their definition, which only constitutes part of the project and of the process.

Among the conditions required for solving problems, Eli de Gortari points out the following: time-lapse to solve them, a correct raising of the problem, that the sought solution does not involve something that is objectively impossible and that the needed methodological tools are available.

These elements help propose a correct project without guaranteeing a solution to the problem.

We can also consider solution conditions derived from Cartesian tradition such as beginning by enunciating the problem, identifying its parts, and acknowledging the essential elements and the manner in which they are related.

It is worth clarifying that it is not necessary to find a list of requirements in order to solve design problems, if it were thus, the solution would be immediate, almost automatic, what's important is to understand the interrelation of the requirements - which is what makes the process complex -, and this way be able to determine the type of work that design demands in each case.

In order to achieve this and following the same Cartesian tradition, moments of the process of solution can be included: *analysis, comparison, contrasting, definition, description, discussion, enumeration, evaluation, exemplification and demonstration.*

The designer must keep in mind that any problem formulation that he faces implicitly carries some reference to the form of solution.

Having defined the design problem, the following step is the methodological structure, known as the design process. Structuring a project consists of detecting the plot or set of fundamental relations that correspond to defined moments, based on a logical sequence.

All these considerations clarify that the complexity of design methodology presumes that the analysis of problems is undoubtedly important, because without it, the process of design would be incoherent, arbitrary and senseless; nevertheless, Bonsiepe is right when affirming that the process, even when based on excellent methods, does not reach the definitive form of the product by itself, it defines and qualifies it, but does not solve it graphically.

The form is contained but must be deciphered and converted into an object, insists the author, who considers that "this conversion process – the true work of design – has up until now constituted the arcane aspect of all methodologies [...] no methodology, not even the most sophisticated [...] has proposed techniques for successfully performing the process of turning an analytical diagram into a form".[36]

Knowing the problems and the process of design does not exhaust the methodology; on the contrary, it only marks the beginning and the incessant need for better methods.

The lack of methodological support and the employment of ambiguous methods that lack theoretical fundamentals result in the designer making absurd solution proposals that not only do not provide benefits to society but, on the contrary, create irrational problems and result in the diversion of technical and human resources in senseless enterprises.

The best proof of the previously mentioned lies in the huge amount of problems whose solutions are allegedly founded in projects, that not only did not become solved, but have created problems that made them insoluble, like the obstruction of terrestrial, maritime and aerial traffic, highways, visual, auditory and conceptual contamination, chronic urban degradation of services, exhaustion of energy resources, etc.

---

36 G. Bonsiepe, *Op. cit.*, p. 29

Necessity

To understand a design need and its value, it is indispensable to consider the contextual characteristics that affect a given object. Basic needs are those that are vital and of subsistence, like food and shelter; however, there are other basic needs, those that are primary through cultural heritage, inseparable from the individual's social development, like for example a bed, trousers, shoes, or transportation, from which emerge the designing of useful objects and images. However, today's society creates needs that transcend the recreational aspect and impact the social level, the vanity, the illusions and the fantasies that are always related to advertising systems, from which emerge ornamental objects, fashion objects and useless objects.

Necessity is the most important motivational factor in the configuration of the environment to which design, of course, is not alien. Is the result of the awareness of some deficiency that, when satisfied, gratifying sensations are produced: enjoyment, pleasure, wellbeing, relaxation, etc. Design satisfies needs that are specified by using objects and the configuration of meanings.

Necessity is *necesitatis* in Latin, name of the constitutive quality of *necessarium*, which comes from *necesse*, what never ceases, never ceases to be. Thence, 'necessary' is the term that indicates that which is and cannot cease to be. The term 'necessary' acquires a meaning of value, which specifies what should be and, extensively, what should be had.

Francisco García Olvera concludes that necessity is "the deficiency or urgency that becomes evident with the demand of what one lacks or wants to be",[37] and what is of interest for design is demand, the demand for a material or formal satisfaction.

If we adopt the hypothesis of the first man and consider his first actions when taking objects and using them we face situations that are inherent to his primary needs and the relevant role of the satisfiers, and so it becomes clear that in order to find food he will design different types of arrows, spears, clubs; to facilitate food ingestion, he will come up with pans, tableware, cutlery; to guarantee his safety, defence items; to protect himself from the weather, clothes and a roof; and finally, for his social life he will start designing symbols with very diverse functions.

Needs are determined by the culture and the civilization and therefore their values and function vary according to the context in which they are given, this way, for example, umbrella and shoes are primary needs in one large city and secondary or non-existent in some African communities.

This means that it is indispensable to consider the contextual characteristics that affect the design of a particular object, because these characteristics determine the necessity and its value. In spite of inherent epistemological difficulties, needs that are considered primary are usually those that are primordial by cultural heredity and are inseparable from the individual's social development, like his bed, trousers, shoes, etc., in contrast with the so-called secondary needs within the same context, like ornamental objects, objects of fashion or useless objects.

What is important is not so much to speak of primary or secondary needs but to understand the limitations that drive man, which can be illustrated by imagining a triangle where the first side represents his

37 Francisco García Olvera. "Design Definition 1" in *Magenta*, No. 2, p. 20

environment, the second is the mental skill that he adopts in order to live in that environment, and the third is the certainty of his mortality. The goal of man's actions is to satisfy the triangle's spheres. Man has fought to adapt his surroundings to his needs, overcoming the difficulties that he encountered, for example, trees that were too tall, excessively long distances, high or low temperatures, etc. and thus has designed tools that allowed for the extension of his limbs.

Abraham Moles classifies needs by regions:

- Vital biological and subsistence needs (food, shelter, etc.)
- Basic social needs
- Needs that come from one's image of oneself concerning social status, self-esteem, vanity, etc.
- Needs for luxury and things given for free, which to a great extent create advertising systems.
- Needs created out of illusions and fantasies.

From a different viewpoint, needs can be classified based on their continuity:

Permanent Vital	***Precise changing***	***Needs that arise from***	***Pure desires***
Needs	Needs (sexuality)	Wishes (eroticism)	(willpower)

Needs can also be classified into material and immaterial, the latter including spiritual and emotional, among which the ones that stand out are: epistemological curiosity or the need to know what has led man to invent or innovate both art and science.

One mustn't forget to include in the classification of needs the role played by man's recreational nature, which has given rise to games like chess, dominoes, and sports, whose function depends on a combination of cultural factors.

Consequently, the classifications are formulated based on specific needs, they must consider the degree of urgency that these needs represent in a specific culture, and this explains how the different forms of design were created:

- *Urbanism* is born out of the need to organize space in human communities.
- *Urban and industrial architecture* is born out of the need to create shelter and protection.
- *Interior design* is born out of the need to organize interior spaces.
- *Industrial design* is born out of the need to produce objects and tools.
- *Graphic design and visual communication* are born out of the need to organize the cultural messages that we perceive through sight.
- *Clothing* – in the broad sense -, and *textile design* – in a more specific sense -, are born out of the need to cover and protect the human body.

Last, we must keep in mind that even though not all needs are satisfied through objects, these do play an important role as satisfiers, which is increased due to the effects of technology, making these objects accessible to more and more people; this fact forces the designer to be alert against the indifference and depersonalization created by industrialization, translated into the employment of mechanistic methodological models that do not consider the user.

If the designer wishes to elevate design to the highest levels of culture, he must acquire the critical conscience that is needed to capture the essential effects that social life produces, only this way will his work be rationally congruent with man's real needs; this involves the development of criteria of values that allow him to pin down priorities, not only specific – related to design – but also general, concerning culture in its sense of a continuous process of human improvement.

User

The user is object and aim of every design action, and in the object or image he loos for nothing more than the fulfilment of his needs.

Man, when forming part of the social system, manifests himself through behaviours that create two different forms of relationships:

- *Human relationships* developed through specific behaviours, word, mimic, gesture, etc.
- *Objectualizing relationships*, given through objects.

The system of objects, which includes references to human needs, integrates a system of significance in which the objects speak of the user, and through them, he seeks for and establishes the order in which he has a place.

The objects are integrated into different types of artifacts that have a functional value determined by the use that they provide to the user. Currently, this is the determinant factor of industrial production which, nevertheless, is based on an abstract conception of the user to whom it is destined.

Only a century ago, the user – or consumer – would tell the artisan what features the object that he wanted must have and if those features were not satisfied, the object would be modified or even substituted. Nowadays, however, objects for daily use are manufactured massively, responding to utilitarian and aesthetic criteria that frequently have nothing to do with the user's – consumer's – needs and tastes.

Currently, the formal synthesis is given in regards to an abstract and universal recipient conceived in the mind of the designer, based on requirements determined by those who induce, persuade or make something necessary and not by those who actually need it.

The production of handicrafts allowed for a personal relationship between the user and the object, "the only freedom that the user has nowadays in regards to industrial products is the possibility to choose between products of different manufacturers and, eventually, the personal modification of the product using stickers and the likes".[38]

In order to make a classification of objects in relation to users, one must consider how the process of using is experienced; what subjective value does it have; what is the appropriation relationship that determines the object's use; what physical, psychic and social factors determine the object's use.

The user is the object and goal of every design action "as long as the user is related to the project through an abstract analysis of the typified needs of a group of users of similar characteristics and not through democratic intervention in the decisions".[39]

---

[38] Bernd Löbach. *Industrial Design*, p. 58

[39] O. Olea, *Op. cit.*, p. 32

Therefore, what the user looks for in the product is no more than the fulfilment of his needs. The producer, however, tries to affect the informative performance in a way that when the object is in the hands of the user, it continues to allow him to exploit him as a determining factor of consumption. It is therefore convenient to state that the user, who is effectively capable of distinguishing what is useful when using it, is incapable of anticipating this.

The designer's creative capacity must allow him to foresee the right instrumental answer that each human collectivity will require, objects that a given society is willing to assume and incorporate into their way of life.[40]

The previous consideration supposes an ideal relationship between user and object, but what is certain is that, currently, the user becomes a slave of mercantile economic structures of the societies of consumption, and is reduced to an abstract entity that will only be manifested as a real being at the moment of use when he would submit the object to the testing of his needs; if this fails, the resulting information will not reach the designer but become lost in the different instances of the process of production.

The modern user, who is more and more far from understanding the production process of the objects that he uses, focuses his attention on the symbol value, which creates his fetishization.

Alienation and fetishization are skilfully used by the producers to their advantage, and they stack the user with objects, even up to a level of over-saturation, because "he needs to discover or awaken new needs in consonance with the goal of economic growth".[41]

Such serious affirmations like that of Löbach must be attended to by the theory of design because it is a fact that the designer has been separated from the public as a consequence of business interests. In

---

[40] A. Ricard, *Op. cit.*, pgs. 70-71

[41] B. Löbach, *Op. cit.*, p. 28

fact, we are living in the paradox in which it more frequently occurs that the user is no longer the seeker.

The designer's indifference to this situation makes it indispensable to insist on the need to rescue the designer-user relationship, whose rupture has resulted in the production of absolute object designs that are seemingly capable of satisfying the abstract needs of a unique and universal user, archetypal, created by an estranged industrial process, which is not only not the image of anybody, inexistent, but also prevents the possibility of being.

The user must be understood as a being with aesthetic and ethical needs and not only as an anthropometrically and statistically measurable object. The integral comprehension of the user should be a requirement for any design project.

Some theoreticians suggest the possibility of an open participative design in which sponsors, designers and users form a cycle that allows for designs that are better adapted to their physical and spiritual needs, so that the object of design implies a real relationship that allows improving life's social conditions.

Creativity

Creativity is like the Voyager Golden Record, containing information and knowledge and navigating aimlessly in space, it has a key and anyone who is interested in its contents (the searcher), may open it and extract files that help understand human beings. And so, creativity is considered a mixture of fantasy and invention, necessarily based on knowledge, on experiences that allow relating in different manners preceding data, thus establishing new realities.

To create, according to the *Dictionary of the Royal Academy of the Spanish Language*, is to 'produce something out of nothing' consequently, it is evident that it would be improper and wrong to speak of the 'creativity' of man, whose work does not begin with the inexistent. However, we speak of creativity when an original and new being is created out of a given reality.

André Ricard says that to create is to contribute something unforeseen, that "we can only speak of creation when the work is innovative, when it offers an original and congruent alternative [...] creativity is feasible because man, in addition to his rationality, also has an affectivity that allows him to capture that which escapes his reason".[42]

In this sense, creativity seems to be considered a strange mix of fantasy and innovation, but necessarily based on knowledge, on experiences that allow relating in different manners preceding information and thus establishing new realities, and so, creative thought involves the adoption of a different point of view. Tudor Powell defines creativity as

> [...] a combination of flexibility, originality and sensitivity to ideas, which enables the thinker to break away from usual sequences of thought into different and productive sequences, the result of which gives satisfaction to himself and possibly to others.[43]

Indeed, every creation is always an elaborate and complex synthesis of what we analyze rationally with what is suggested by the intuition that results of man's innate tendency to search for the pleasure that its produces.

The capacity to create is innate to the human condition and can be manifested in any field of his task. Since the day he is born, man records in his mind either consciously or unconsciously meaningful images and information that he keeps in his memory, a condition necessary for the reflection that allows inference, that is, to establish a series of possibilities and choices that are different to the already given ones.

---

[42] A. Ricard, *Op. cit.*, p. 213

[43] Tudor Powell Jones quoted by Elba Carrillo. "Creativity" in *Educational Profiles*, No.1, p. 32

In this process, the role played by analogy stands out. Analogy is a form of inductive logical reasoning that, through reason, allows us to find similarities in the differences, and it is known as one of the main factors of creative capacity. However, the springs of creativity are yet to be explained and this could not be otherwise, for if it were and a method for creativity were to be found, *its essence, which is originality, would disappear and in stead of creation we would have reproduction.*

The impossibility to establish a method for creativity does not prevent, however, the acknowledgement of a group of skills that makes it possible:

- *Sensitivity* toward the problems.
- *Fluidity*, or facility to use knowledge when faced with new or unexpected situations (verbal, ideative, figurative, semantic, symbolic, associative and expressive).
- *Flexibility* to tackle the same problem in different manners.
- *Originality* referred to a personal way of doing and thinking which results in unpredictable answers.
- *Ability* to produce, for it is not enough to create new ideas, it is also necessary to develop and carry them out.
- *Discipline*, consisting of the capacity for order and persistence in the work.
- The X factor, the imponderable of *Creativity*.

The creative process supposes making a choice between options in which reason and imagination are combined to materialize specifically in what is created. Its complexity is such that it is not always cognoscible even by the creator himself. There are innumerable examples in art and science of creations that are not comprehensible by their authors, even when considering chance, which often plays an important role. In this regard, Bertrand Russell's testimony is eloquent:

> [...] I needed a period of sub-conscious incubation which could not be hurried and was, if anything, impeded by deliberate thinking [...] having, through a time of very intense concentration, raised the problem in my subconscious, it would

> germinate underground until, suddenly, the solution emerged with blinding clarity.[44]

What stands out in this testimony is the moment of illumination, emerging suddenly and with no explanation after periods of confusion in which the hypotheses and efforts prove futile until the ideas all of a sudden become clear.

Einstein, on the other hand, acknowledged that imagination is more important than knowledge, but that it is not given without it.

It must be clarified that illumination is not for free and even though it has not always been an object of precise explanation, it always presents itself as the result of intellectual and emotional factors that stake the acquired experiences and knowledge and a certain dominion in the field of the activity in which the creation is given.

Creative capacity operates similarly in all the periods of history and areas of culture, the variants are given as a result of the material contents and finalities.

In the same manner in which creative making is given in two levels, inspiration and reflection, which suppose the control of reason over intuition, we can also speak of the degrees in which it is given:

- *Expression,* first level, characterized by its spontaneity and independence of stereotypes and conventionalisms.
- *Production,* related to the concretion of the process of realization, which exhibits the author's mastery of his subject.
- *Discovery or invention,* consisting of the novelty contributed by the creation, or where appropriate, the *innovation,* if the result is the work of a restructuring of the known elements, in a way that what is already given is renewed through original process and method. This category includes what Thomas Kuhn calls knowledge revolution due to the change of paradigms.

---

[44] Noted in Hubert Jaoui. *Clefs pour la créativité,* p. 63

- *Emersion,* attributed to a creation that is considered genial like the kind that contributes something radically new and unknown, capable of changing cultural parameters in a given time period, for example, Einstein's theory of relativity.

From all this we can conclude that creative capacity is manifested as:

- Association of ideas or mental process, a new combination of ideas
- An activity in which the ideative process is linked to inspiration.
- Skill for restructuring patterns of relationship in an innovative manner.

Creative capacity, as all other human aptitudes, has its own limits, personal as well as social, biological and cultural, in a way that it cannot be separated from historical conditions nor from the material relations of existence.

All these principles and criteria are valid in design; design cannot be a product of mere intuition, imagination or sensitivity with no order, it always requires a methodological order, reflection and knowledge. Creative capacity does not emerge out of emptiness or ignorance; it is only given where there is reason and imagination integrated by the goals that the designer pursues and coherence in the employment of the means and resources that he has access to, according to the nature of his objects and the needs that he looks to satisfy.

In spite of the fact that, according to what has been affirmed, no methodological norm can explain how a creative moment is given, as it is unique in its plot and in itself, the conditions that make creativity possible in design demand their own specificity provided by methodology, given that their result involves man and his needs, and so this carries a complex network of functional requirements.

Form – Function

The value of functions varies in a way that if, for example, the practical aspect predominates, then there is a ***practical-functional configuration****, like* *the case of the dining chair on the Shaker communities in New Lebanon, USA, 1890 industrial design, or Félix Beltrán's Click poster. If the symbolic aspect predominates, then there is a* **symbolic-functional configuration***, as in the case of the Barcelona Chair, produced in 1928 by Ludwig Mies Van der Rohe for the German Pavilion at the 1929 Barcelona Exposition or the 1982 Soccer World Cup set of posters in Barcelona. Finally, when the aesthetic aspect predominates, then there is an* **aesthetic-functional configuration***, which is mostly given in the industrial field, in the area of visual perception; such is the case of G.T. Rietveld's armchair painted in red, blue, black and yellow in 1917, considered more of an art object than a useful one, a case similar to that of Chris Kluge's Music Insects of the World poster*

Valladolid
COPA DEL MUNDO DE FUTBOL ESPAÑA 82
Madrid 1982
COPA DEL MUNDO DE FUTBOL ESPAÑA 82
MÁLAGA
COPA DEL MUNDO DE FUTBOL ESPAÑA 82
ZARAGOZA
COPA DEL MUNDO DE FUTBOL ESPAÑA 82
sevilla
COPA DEL MUNDO DE FUTBOL ESPAÑA 82
1982
Valencia
COPA DEL MUNDO DE FUTBOL ESPAÑA 82

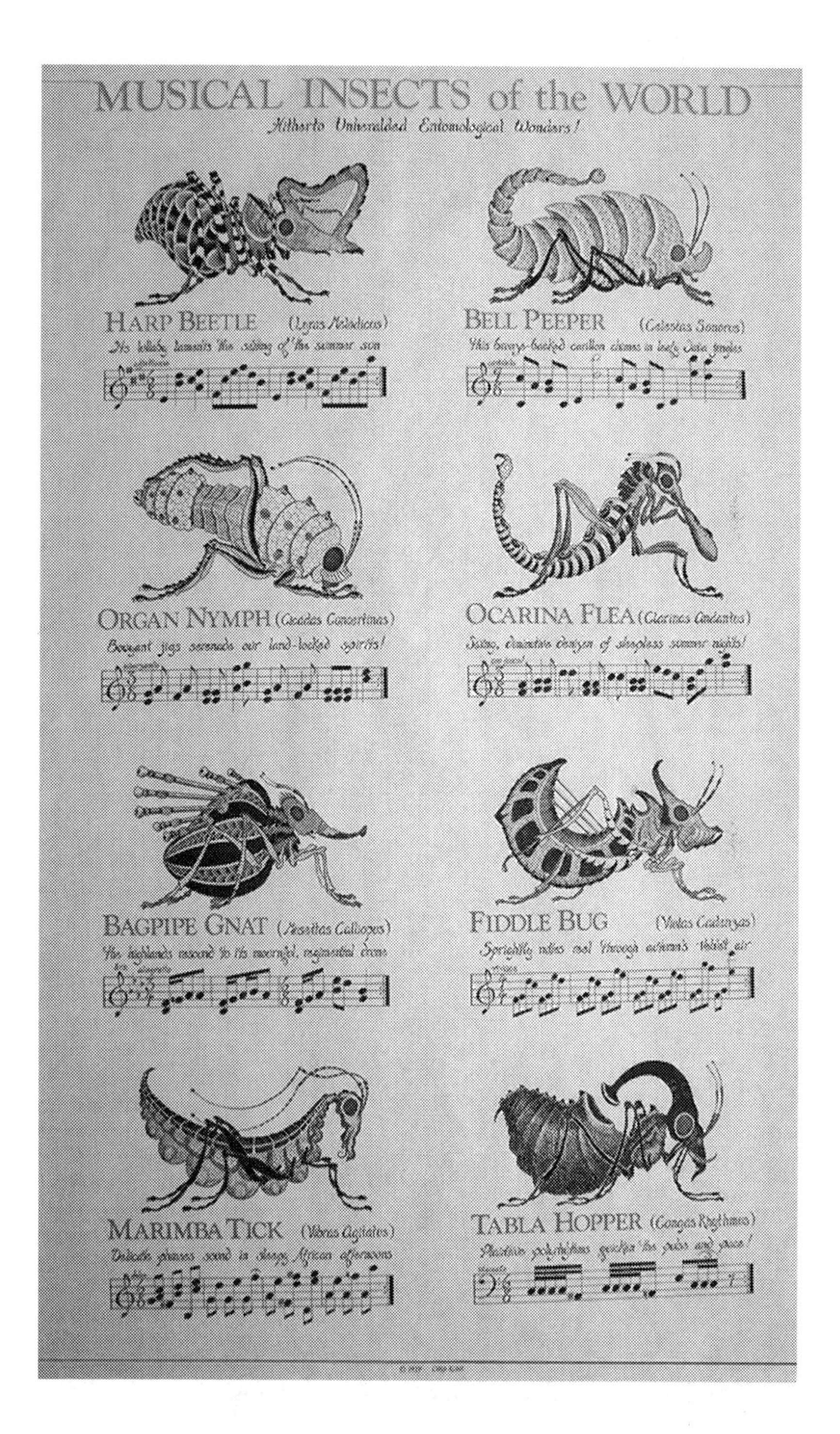
MUSICAL INSECTS of the WORLD
Hitherto Unheralded Entomological Wonders!
HARP BEETLE
BELL PEEPER
ORGAN NYMPH
OCARINA FLEA
BAGPIPE GNAT
FIDDLE BUG
MARIMBA TICK
TABLA HOPPER

ORGÁNICOS
ORGÁNICOS

The task of design consists of configuring, giving a form to objects; however, since this involves a direct relationship with man, the task is conditioned in a way that it is not about merely giving form just for the sake of it, but also defining it based on usefulness. Endowing the objects with the peculiar and specific configuration that allows improving their function as tools, their service and their relationship with man: that is the designer's task.

The designer must project in a coherent manner the disposition of the elements that will be submitted to the user's perception; thus, he is basically considered an organizer of structures.

The design process is determined by formal coherence, which involves both the functional and operative resolution as well as the visual form.

Form is inherent to objects. Every tangible entity possesses physical presence that is nothing but the matter's exterior determination, whose form is subordinate to the service for which it is destined.

The daily object – car, telephone, stove, signboard, road sign, etc. – is a carrier of forms, of Gestalt – to say it in psychological terms -. According to Abraham Moles, objects are carriers of morphemes that are united in a certain order, individually recognizable, combinable based on general demands: topology, continuity, materiality, and so the *object itself is a communication because its form is a message that precedes its materiality*.

Form, final set of elements that are demanded for their function, associated with the operative attitude or aptitude and emits a visual message that influences the synchronic consideration of the whole.

The visual message of objects must not be ignored because it defines their role as a means of communication on different levels: as a carrier of forms, as mediator in interindividual relationships, as a transmitting agent in the culture of the objects, as an indicator of property and social status, etc.

The formal coherence of the visual message is technically based on the way the elements are distributed; this way, *isomorphic* is that which employs equal elements, for example, a modular construction (same form, same dimensions); *homeomorphic* is that which exhibits different dimensions with equal forms; and *catamorphic* is that which is integrated by different not-exactly-equal dimensions but recognizable by the interfigural relation.

The order of the formal elements is called structure, and "if we arrange these elements according to a criterion or viewpoint and assign a finality, we will have what is called a system",[45] it can be said that structure is nothing but the materialization of the system.

In addition to the technical factor that defines an object's configuration, there is the context, which the designer does not control and to which the form must be adapted.

The designer must search for adjustment between *form* and *context*, which is understood as "the place in which the object is located; the use that will be made of it; the production methods, etc [...] all that is outside the designer's area [...] where he begins and what the design must be adapted to".[46]

Every form is given in an atmosphere with which it establishes a series of relationships in order to form the environment in which the form is conditioned according to the new semiotic field that is originated; there, it acquires new and different meanings that it does not posses when isolated.

It is considered that the context or surroundings are the parts of the tangible world that determine the form. The solution to a design problem begins with the coherence between form and context, and must satisfy the demands of both in such a way that the resulting object coexists with its surroundings, and effortlessly manages to have contact with them. *The environment defines the problem, the form solves it.*

---

[45] F. García Olvera, *Op. cit.*, p. 21

[46] Xavier Rupert de Ventós, *Op.cit.*, p. 9

When an object's context changes, the form remains inalterable but the use given to it and the meaning attributed to it may be different, depending on the cultural patterns. This way, for example, a drum that for some ethnic groups is simply a means of communication, for others, it is a musical instrument or an ornamental object.

Objects, based on their functional interpretation, integrate the expression of cultures in the so-called object complex or functional unit, which refers to interrelations of time and space among objects.

The formal and functional confrontation among objects creates a permanent economic desire according to which the forms that resolve this with best technical quality survive, that is, the forms that are better integrated to the objects' functions tend to remain: the needle, the axe, the sickle, all of which are instruments whose minimal intrinsic formal qualities determine their durability.

An object's long-term usefulness depends on its morphological competence. In simple implements, the form's interdependence, its use and materials are evident for the best configuration to be made; this way, for example, we have the funnel or the screw, or – in a different scope – symbols such as the Red Cross. All these cases manifest the precise correspondence between form and function.

Graphic designs and objects are presented as functional units where it is possible to separate the concurrent elements and moments of the creative composition, because it has been said that design is a synthesis of the form that solves a structure.

An object's final structure follows its function, sometimes reaching it, as in the above-mentioned examples; other times the form evolves following a slow process of adaptation through which the object is stabilized in its environment or is eliminated. Morphology is subject to adaptation:

> [...] throughout the generations, a species will alter its form in order to better adapt itself to the innumerable circumstances that integrate its surroundings and the life that it carries

> inside them: its performance [...] the form of an object will obey the needs of its function.[47]

Jean Baudrillard, in *Critique of the Political Economy of the Sign*, affirms that the form-function harmonious synthesis corresponds to the fundamental theory of design and to what he calls the aesthetic logic of objects. One of the problems that this author mentions about this theory is that designers -when elaborating partial theses regarding the progressive development of form in search for the environment's supposed ideal state-, disguise and shelter sign functions in the formal innovation, that acquire processes of cultural discrimination through the objects.

It is clear that one of design's determinations is its functional value, which results from the relationship between needs and human skills.

It is worth clarifying that function is specified from many points of view: what it does, how it operates, how it changes, how long it lasts, how it is adapted, etc., all these depending on the psychological and social factors that determine the needs.

From this we conclude that in order to look at an object and examine its function it is necessary to consider the historical moment.

The concept of function contributes to the comprehension of the surrounding objects and the transformation of these surroundings; therefore, it is a constant of every methodological process: in every design project, one should consider the physical, psychological and technological elements that correspond to the objects' functions. Their suitability will be determined by the fulfilment of the user's needs.

Even though functional structure responds to a combination of elements, designed with the purpose of providing a determined action, the designer adds to the object aesthetic and symbolic functions which,

---

[47] Christopher Williams. *Form Origins*, p. 76

when not establishing a balance with the structure, may lead to a mediatization if the practical function and result in fashion or styling.

The synthetic nature of design is manifested in the necessary integration of the structural and functional complexities. The functional complexity includes:

- Practical aspects related to product-user relationships;
- Aesthetic aspects concerning a subjective evaluation deriving from the perception that includes considerations regarding colour, surface, sound, texture, dimensions, etc.;
- Symbolic aspects concerning the objects' semantic field.

The value of the functions varies in a way that if, for example, the practical aspect predominates, then one is in the presence of a practical-functional configuration, as was the case of the *dining chair* of the Shaker communities in New Lebanon, USA, 1890 industrial design, or Félix Beltrán's Click poster.

When the symbolic aspect predominates, one is in the presence of a symbolic-functional configuration, as in the case of the *Barcelona Chair* designed in 1928 by Ludwig Mies Van der Rohe for the German Pavilion at the 1929 Barcelona Exposition or the *1982 Soccer World Cup set of posters* in Spain.

Finally, when the aesthetic aspect predominates, one is in the presence of an aesthetic-functional configuration, which is most often given in the industrial field, in the area of visual perception; such is the case of G.T. Rietveld's *armchair painted in red, blue, black and yellow* in 1917, considered more of an art object than a practical one, a case similar to that of Chris Kluge's *Music Insects of the World* poster.[48]

None of these functions escapes the human shallowness that is manifested in different forms through the history of the cultures. In our days, there are innumerable examples of futile, superfluous, useless,

[48] However, it must be clear that the aesthetic value must answer first to the function and not to the designer's expressive need.

extravagant, snobbish designs that are many a time destined to be symbols of prestige, admiration, scandal, social status, etc.

Consequently, one of the difficulties that designers, either industrial or graphic, are faced with is avoiding these deformations and giving the proper answer to the objective demands of use and the subjective possibilities of the formal expression, because it is not about decorating or putting make-up on the objects, like styling does; the designer's goal should be to achieve the formal cohesion of the objects according to their context.

The designer is responsible for defining the configuration and its effects according to a methodological process that he must include to that effect:

- The requirements of the action that he intends to obtain.
- The demand that its use will require.
- The limitations of the technology used.
- The meaning that, as a symbol, the form will acquire in its cultural context.

When the formal and functional demands are founded on an indissoluble whole, when the configuration is that which is required by the use, the design "achieves an aesthetic value per se. This orthomorphism is – beyond fashion – the dominion over the formal harmony and serenity that emerge through the apparent surface of the form, from the depth of its own reason";[49] even when an orthomorphism, to which only anthropogenic things that last can enter, is not obtained, every object must tend toward formal pertinence which is coherent with its own essence.

---

[49] A. Ricard, *Op. cit.*, p. 178

THEORETICAL PRINCIPLES OF DESIGN

Theory of objects

An object is not a natural being in the same way that a stone or a tree is; the later are things, an object emerges from the transformation of objects by man's doing; it is the work of ***Homo faber****, a permanent counterpart of* ***Homo otiosus****. The system of objects, as a group of morphological relationships, syntactic articulations and semantic correspondences, is manifested as a symbolic world of which social identification and interpretation go beyond mere usefulness. The designer must keep in mind the value of causality and finality of the world of objects, since they play a fundamental historical role in the survival and evolution of Homo sapiens.*

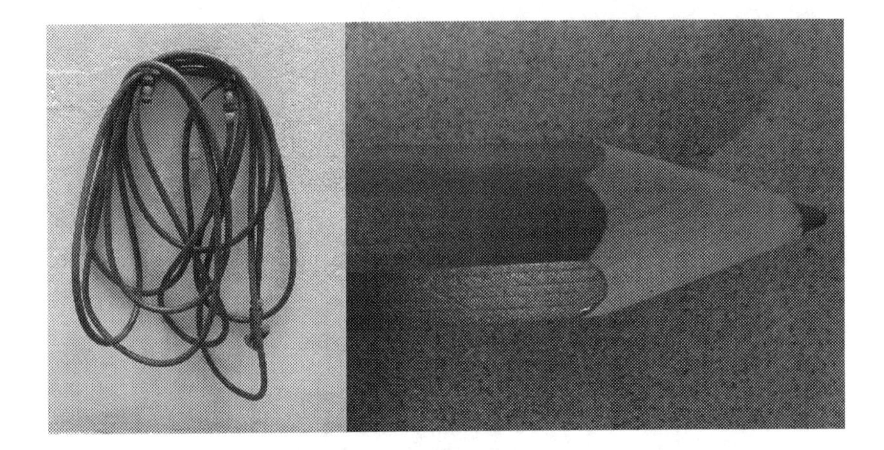

The environment is defined as all of that which surrounds an individual in space and time; the following two categories stand out:

- *Nearby environment* or all that is within immediate reach.
- *Distant environment* or that which involves movement or wait.

The human environment is the scene in relation to which one lives in inclusion or reclusion but, in any case, it is a place of action. It is a receptacle but also a product, created, invented, constructed, fabricated, transformed, etc. by human beings.

Culture's sphere is the environment, which is the result of the always-recommencing task of giving sense to the world. The man-created environment is culture in the sense that, in it, symbols and values of objects and situations are fixed and interpreted.

In the environment, the object acts as essential mediator of the social body; it is a communicator of masses in that it is a carrier of symbols and values (a progressive step is created from the function object to the communication object), and therefore it must be considered "in its selection, its organization and its practice, as the support of a global structure of the environment [...] an active structure of behaviour",[50] here, Roland Barthes suggests the possibility of the so-called philosophy of the object, destined to reflect on its being and place it on display.

---

50 Cfr. Roland Barthes. *Semiotics Adventure*, pp. 245-255

The object, considered a designed entity, takes us back to the object's and the design's environments. The latter, in which the first is configured, supposes that objects are an element of connection between man and nature, an element of connection among men, and carriers of a bonus of meaning or what has been denominated symbol value, that allows them to function as connotators.

As a whole, the system of object relations constitutes their phenomenology.

Etymologically, *objectum* means thrown against, something that exists outside of us, something placed before us with a material nature: all that is offered to the sight and affects the senses; some philosophers use the term in the epistemological sense of what is being thought as opposed to the subject who thinks it.

Abraham Moles, in *Theory of objects*, defines objects as "elements of the outer world, fabricated by man and which he can grab or manipulate [...] they are independent and movable [...] they have a character that is submitted to man's will".[51]

It must be emphasized that an object is not a natural being in the sense of a stone or a tree, the object emerges out of the transformation of objects by the action of man; it is the work of the *Homo faber,* a permanent counterpart of the *Homo otiosus.*

The system of objects, as a group of morphological relationships, syntactic articulations and semantic correspondences, is manifested as a symbolic world whose social identification and interpretation go beyond mere usefulness.

The analysis of isolated objects has no sense but as statistical data, their evaluation must be understood as a product of their structural relationships, in relation to the perspectives of the projects to which they belong, and determined according to the circumstances of their existence.

---

[51] Abraham Moles. *Objects Theory*, p. 32

When considering the anthropogenic nature (neologism formed by *anthropos*: man and *genon*: foetus) of the world of objects, one must keep in mind its aspect of causality and finality, since objects play an historical role that is fundamental for the survival and evolution of *Homo sapiens.*

The influence of objects on the development of language is obvious, given that from the moment in which they become part of everyday life they require a man to identify them.

The denomination of objects is given in relation to their use, and we can distinguish criteria that serve as reference to their name and impact on the development of language, thus we have:

- Objects whose names have created verbs: button/ to button, nail/ to nail, fusil/ to fusillade, etc.
- Objects from which no verbs have been derived: basin, chair, plate, book, etc.
- Objects named according to the material that they are made of: paper, glass, cork, etc.
- Objects named based on the product that they contain: sugar bowl, oilcan, milk carton, fishbowl, etc.
- Objects whose name describes their function: sharpener, lightning conductor, lamp socket, lock, dish rack, squeezer, etc.
- Objects whose names are neologisms formed by the combination of Greek and Latin etymologies: automobile, telephone, periscope, etc.

The wide variety of objects has motivated researchers of different specialties to attempt to make classifications that will allow the methodical study of these objects, among these and only with the aim of illustrating, are Andre Ricard's, who classifies objects based on their degree of complexity and their function:

- *Simple*, which have no mechanical device and act as a monolithic whole, they imitate, substitute or extend some part of the human morphology, like a comb, tweezers, plate, hammer, knife, etc.
- *Articulate* or structures like a complex of pieces that are combined to perform a specific function, like scales, pliers, and scissors.

- *Machines,* distinguished from the articulate because they do not require human energy to function, like a boiler, blender, washing machines, car.

Bernd Löbach, on the other hand, classifies objects into four categories:

- *Natural*, created without man's participation (according to a different denomination than the one considered herein, because he considers things as objects).
- *Natural modified by man.*
- *Artistic*, designed to satisfy aesthetic preferences.
- *For use*, destined to satisfy needs.

In regards to the latter, he distinguishes: *products of consumption,* which are exterminated after their use, i.e. food-related; of *individual use* which include feathers, pens, eyeglasses, etc.; of *collective use* such as furniture, refrigerator, television, telephone, apartment, transport, etc. and of *industrial use* including motors, turbines, installations, etc.

In fact, every author can try the formulation of different classifications according to very varied criteria, in such a way that it is evident that the classifications, in the best scenario, have a didactic and illustrative orientation, that they may serve as a guide according to the specific objectives of each author, but in no way can they be understood as methodological criteria because none of them can argue in their favour any fundament of legitimacy.

In this sense, Baudrillard's consideration is pertinent, stating that in spite of the fact that form, material, colour, duration, use, spatiality, etc. are constitutive elements of the object's code, actually it is the individuals and the groups who configure its particular repertoire and give it "the same use as to any moral or institutional code [...] they employ it in their own way: they play with it, cheat with it and speak in its dialect of class ".[52]

---

[52] Jean Baudrillard. *Crítica de la economía política del signo*, p. 13

Finally, he acknowledges that a sociological analysis of the objects is necessary to establish a theory of the objects, but he clarifies that it requires, in addition to structural analyses, political-ideological analyses because of the social function that they fulfil.

Theory of Value

The value of objects should be proportional to the fulfilment of needs; however, the current and prevailing concepts in the market economy promote the adjudging of a value of change to objects, consisting of their market price as merchandise, in addition to their value of use that is conditioned by their function and their material qualities. Likewise, social relations have sharpened the value of sign or symbolic value of objects, which increase their value of change. Based on this we can distinguish between a knife grinder's bicycle, a Saab bicycle whose price is reachable only by a high social status, and examples like the first bicycle or the one used by Alexander Vinokurov in the Tour de France, both of which have such strong symbolic change that they have become museum pieces.

The designer's task is an activity that is subject to economic factors and, therefore, responds to the laws of *production, distribution and consumption.* Consequently, a sociological theory of objects must be based on the social relations created by the economic exchange, in which one must not lose sight of the importance of competition, consumerism and social stratification.

The spontaneous and quotidian vision of the objects must improve itself based on economic needs, priority of use and acquisition of sense, which dependent on the environment, in such a way that the systems of objects correspond to the different social groups; there emerges the object's character of mediator between the individuals and the social reality.

The designer constantly faces pressures due to the producers' economic aims and these frequently create an apparent reality, which at the same time creates the belief of false needs whose fulfilment demands new objectives.

Therefore, the social effects of design require studies that determine their real values of use and the value of the work that they involve.

Behind every object, there is a process of value that, in addition to its value of usefulness, is a term of a social process of economic value.

From the moment in which objects fulfil the real or apparent needs of socially conditioned users, they acquire the character of *commodity*.

As a commodity, objects respond to a given manner of production, to a specific type of social relations, to a special form of communication, and the result is translated into a form of graphic or industrial design that includes the concept of work as a process of transformation that generates wealth and is consequently included in the system of social values.

In order to conduct an analysis of objects as a commodity, one must begin with the theses of classical economy related to value and, therefore, refer to the contributions of Karl Marx, who defined it as "an external object, a thing which through its qualities satisfies human needs of whatever kind. The nature of these needs, whether they arise, for example, from the stomach, or the imagination, makes no difference. Nor does it matter here how the thing satisfies man's need".[53]

Of course, one must keep in mind all the studies dedicated to the development of economy and especially the current and prevailing ideologies related to the market's economy; however, the current contributions do not alter in any way the double consideration of commodity due to its *value of use* and its *value of change*.

The utility gives objects their value of use, conditioned by their material qualities.

The value of use is the material support of the value of change, which consists of the value given to the commodity in its social relationships; in the same way in which the value of use refers to quality, the value of change refers to quantity.

The value of change dispenses with the value of use and this allows understanding why useless objects acquire an enormous value of change in certain social circles, and the consequences of consumerism.

With the disappearance of usefulness from the value of change, the work that is invested in the production of the commodity is eliminated, giving way to an abstract idea of the human work spent on the commodity.

However, this is no reason to stop considering that every value of use represents an amount of work time that is socially necessary in normal conditions – in regards to skill and intensity – of production and work prevailing in a society that determines its magnitude.

The problem in the magnitude of the value is that it remains if there is a constant relationship between the time of duration and the time of work; but if the productive capacity of the work changes and is maintained at the same time, then the magnitude is modified.

---

[53] Carlos Marx, *Op. cit.*, p. 3

Another aspect to consider in relation to objects as commodities lies in that the values of use are not considered individually but in regards to their dimension. Because of their value of change, objects that are made commodities transfer their value of use from one pair of hands to another and thus satisfy social needs, the need for change of useful objects.

In principle, the theory of value considers it as determined by the work; the greater the productive capacity, the shorter the time needed for the production of a commodity, the lesser the amount of work and, therefore, the lower the value. On the other hand, the lesser the productive capacity, the more the work that is required and, therefore, the higher the value.

This way, the size of a commodity's value changes parallel to the amount and opposite to the productive capacity of the work that is invested in it. Nevertheless, the psychological theories of value and the complexities of the contemporary economy, the effects of advertising, speculation, etc. have made this thesis at best only a point of reference that may not be accepted but cannot be ignored.

In order for the products to confront each other as commodities, they must be qualitatively different objects of use according to the principles of social division of the work as a condition of industrial production.

The objects of design can be considered, from the point of view of the theory of value, commodities in that they have values of use and of change to which the theoreticians of design add the *value of symbol*, considered as that through which the object acquires a surplus of meaning that connotes status, defines taste, etc. qualitatively different than the value of use, which has been considered a type of *aesthetic added value*.

The objects of design are carriers of meaning because they express not only a useful function but also life habits, levels of income, academic formation, etc., and so they are considered expressions of status adverting to accessory function that fulfil accessory needs, "one finds the impression with valuable materials [...] new aesthetic elements [...]

the value of novelty, the rareness of the product, the difficulty to find it, its high price ".[54]

The values of the objects' symbols, even more so than the values of use and of change, allow understanding that due to the desire for social prestige that is inherent in the personality, the load of symbols contained in the objects bears witness as to who is whom in society.

The object's symbolic surplus acquires more relevance in consumer societies where the value of symbol more and more frequently loses relationship with the value of use.

Because they are carriers of different messages, *objects are considered polysemous and constitute a differentiated system, a grammar, a language* whose possibilities allow multiple interpretations of social phenomena, and this is why objects acquire independence, their own identity that grants them a social value of their own and presents them to the eyes of those who enjoy them away from the social relationships that create them.

The value of symbol of objects is objectified in a way that it makes invisible the social causes that create them, it offers the consumer such an appealing aspect that it makes it seem as if there were nothing behind them, that is, it fetishizes them.

In *fetishes*, the user loses conscience of the object's dimension and values because he cannot arrange them hierarchically and, consequently, it is the fetish's value of symbol that will guide his actions.

The social importance of values lies in that they are the ones that guide relationships and development; consequently, design remains subject to value judgments on which not only the designed object will depend, but also the designer's attitude faced with the different ontological and epistemological, logical and axiological currents of design.

---

[54] B. Löbach, *Op. cit.*, p. 95

In regards to the designer's value of symbol, Baudrillard has formulated the guidelines of what would be a logic of symbol related to the functional aspects of the value of use, economic aspects of the value of change, of the symbolical change and of the value/symbol.[55]

The *functional logic of the value of use* includes the practical operations of design, the *logic of the value of change* refers to the exchange relations, it is a logic of the market; the *logic of symbolic change* refers to the value differences of the exchange and the *logic of value/symbol* refers to the forms of determining social status. According to these logical guidelines, the object is respectively considered a tool, a commodity, a symbol and a sign.

From the outline made herein of the theory of value in design we infer the need for a social theory of design that will include ethical principles that will guide the designer, who must make decisions faced with "the progressive dissolution of the values of use through the irrational relationship between use and designed product, the man's growing alignment of his cosmic surroundings, the fetishization of consumer objects thanks to the collaboration of design".[56]

---

55 J. Baudrillard, *Op. cit.*, p. 57

56 G. Selle, *Op. cit.*, p. 27

Theory of Communication

Every object communicates a sense, that is, a set of meanings, which are manifested in material, structural and sociocultural attributes. In different ways, the function determines the sense, which determines the message that is communicated. This process in not linear and always gives way to the creation of communication networks; for example, bicycles have been diversified in their functions, requiring their own parking spaces or lanes, likewise, a system of graphic communication has been created for their identification and artists and designers have not been indifferent to the possibility of shaping them in a strictly plastic fashion.

Every design object, whether it is architectonic, industrial or graphic, is interpretable by the recipients because it always carries a message and is consequently part of a process of communication that, if it were ignored, it would impede a clear conception of the design. *Design is also communication.*

The communicational role of design lies in its transforming capacity, belongs to its informative capacity, both of visual as well as verbal languages, and is expressed in the *dialogic relationship that is formed between the issuer and the receptor.*

The public is not only a receptor that establishes a merely physical perceptual relationship with the object, its relationship with it is intellectual, the public is receptor and therefore, because it interprets the message through decoding its language, both objective as well as subjectively, design involves a process of intersubjective socialization through the object.

The process of communication includes different aspects: technological, esthetical, economical, political and ideological, and these last ones, by acting as "social cement", are the ones that allow balance.

The act of communication not only depends on the certainty of the form or images, its social responsibility includes the content of the messages. This way, the objects take on different roles as means of communication:

- They are *carriers of form*, visual or tactile sensitizers that prepare reactions and stimulate motor reflexes, it is an elemental message.
- They are *occasions for intersubjective contact*, carriers of functional and symbolic messages whose language responds to personal activities.
- They are *value matter* that stimulates or obstructs ways of thinking and reacting, they propitiate originality or triviality, alignment or dominion.

The sociological thought applied to the communicative meaning of design has given way, among the dominant currents, to:

1. Functionalism, derived from the viewpoint according to which society fulfils its needs through institutions. Its main concepts are *equilibrium* and *conflict*, because every society tends towards the first and attempts to eliminate the second.

   A central problem in functionalism is a conflict called *disfunctionality*, because the greater the disfunctionality, the greater the disequilibrium, considering that society is considered an organism in which all social members adequately fulfil their role.

   In regards to communication, a problem that is yet to be solved in functionalism is that which is related to the *answer*, because it does not clarify why, if institutions are created to satisfy their social needs, many are conditioned – if not created – along with their answers. In this regards, the *manipulation of needs* and *the assimilation relationship: control of the answer* are important.

   The assimilation relationship indicates the manner in which the present social system absorbs through the media messages that it considers dysfunctional, decontextualizes them, unrealizes them, takes away meaningful intensity and makes them innocuous for the system (ex.: the hippie movement); its role of assimilation consists of taking what is peripheral and spreading it as essential (long hair, slogans, flowers, songs, etc.) in such a way that the disfunctionality becomes part of the normality.

   Another subject that has to do with functionalism is *noise*, understood as all external and internal alterations to the mean of communication that distort the message that is broadcasted and must be eliminated. This theory distinguishes *semantic noise* (the communicator has elaborated the message incorrectly), *mechanical noise* (interference is produced during the broadcasting), and *perceptual noise* (the percipient decodes wrongly).

   Linked to this sociological current according to which the referential function is subordinated to others in such a way that the broadcasting, diffusion and reception of the message can be emphasized putting aside its content, M. McLuhan's theory of communication becomes exceptionally important, and its slogan "the means is the message" synthesizes it.

According to this author, who considers the media functional extensions of man, what is essential does not lie in the particular messages that are transmitted but in the social repercussions or guidelines that their operation creates. This means that, for example, it does not matter what TV channel is being watched, but that society watches television and changes its behaviour standards due to television.

2. Structuralism. Tightly linked to functionalism, many structuralist currents have been developed with ideological orientations as dissimilar as those of T. Parsons and L. Strauss, which, nevertheless, have in common *the understanding of the social phenomena based on the formal relationships, that is, the structures in which they are developed.* The *relationships* that are formed *between structure and function* are those that have originated studies that combine both currents, in the so-called *structural-functionalism.*

   The *structural analysis* starts with the tissue of relationships through which the objects are broken down with the objective of finding out their rules of integration and, if that were the case, their operation.

   Structuralism in communication starts with the rules of combination (syntax) that make possible the messages in order to make them comprehensible; this theoretic conception includes the likes of Algirdas J. Greimas, Roland Barthes, Eco, etc.

   In the theory of communication, structuralism focuses on the code and the message, and from their analysis results the reconstruction of the reality that is identified with the created structures, that is, based on the study of rules of relationship that do not include society's material contents, the structural analysis pretends to create a total reality, in other words, endow the pure structures with material content.

In linguistic terms, structuralism sets syntax before semantics, making the latter depend on the first. In this direction, the theories of Ash, Markov and Shannon are included. This way, for example, languages are Markov systems according to which the probability of a sign in a message is determined by the previous sign, as in the case of Spanish, in which after the letter '*m*', a vowel is more likely to follow than a consonant.

Based on Saussure's structuralism, different branches of social sciences have been developed along with different currents of communication, which have attempted to surpass the formal limitations of structuralism and, for that purpose, integrate the material aspects of reality, as is the case of Levi Strauss, who sets the guidelines of a structuralism linked to dialectic materialism with the peculiarity that this tendency leads to the impossibility of integrating all the social structures in a total and unique system.

3. Historical materialism. In spite of the discredit into which it has fallen in the last decade due to the dissolution of the USSR and the failure of the so-called historical socialism, it is beyond question that the epistemological contributions provided by historical materialism have influenced and still influence both the study of design as well as the creations of designers, because it is beyond doubt that the messages have a meaning in relation to the real conditions of existence and the ideological baggage of issuers as well as recipients.

For the analysis of communication in design, the concepts of *structure* and *superstructure*, and within the latter, *ideology*, are very important, because the message in design is always given on a superstructure level, determined by the economical structure, which varies not only according to the manner of production, but also to the influence of the dominant superstructure (think, for example, of the meaning of the religious images in the 18th or 20th centuries).

Ideology, in accordance with historical materialism, is always an intellectual conception based on the position that it holds in the social relationships and always involves a form of deceit that it hides in the images, ideas, designs, the material source that determines them, and the interests to which they respond, so that the ideas appear as separate from the economic interests to which they respond. This way we can understand, for example, how through movies the image of the Nazis or Mexicans is designed in Hollywood.

Design, in accordance with the principles of historical materialism, should reveal through its messages the class interests that originate them so that instead of serving as a form of ideological concealment, they awaken social consciousness, denouncing, if that were the case, exploitation, injustices, etc. in the form of objective expressions of reality.

The outline of the characteristics of the currents of thought that are most influential on communication, among which the *theory of systems, theory of reception* and *hermeneutics* can also be included, and which of course require an approach to their specific aspects, makes evident the importance of the relationship between communication and design, which the designer must approach in two-ways; first, in relation to his knowledge of the different currents of thought and his social influence, and second, in relation to the effects of the design depending on the message that it carries.

The language of design must start, in any case, from the thorough comprehension that objects do not only have a functional meaning but also an informative and formative one, which plays an important role in understanding reality.

The objects of design are carriers of language; they should be studied as signs, and as signs they remain inserted in the mass media.

A *sign*, according to Pierre Guiraud's definition, constitutes a stimulus according to which a mental image is associated with another that is evoked by the sign in order to establish a communication.

Understanding the meanings of the signs can only be accomplished through knowledge of the *codes*, which are always '*necessary conventions*' that allow issuers and recipients to understand their relationship with the objects. In monosemous signs – which have a single meaning – the relationship is simple; but in polysemous signs –in which one word acquires several meanings – the complexity is increased.

The *polysemous nature of a language* includes values that are merely descriptive that claim objectivity (denotation), subjective, ethical, esthetical, and religious values in which the poetic aspect of design is founded (connotation) and values tending toward action can be included.

The values of symbol are studied in three different levels:

1. *Of the word,* related to the analysis of the formal properties (typology and material). It is the syntactic study in that its material is formed by the signs' characteristics without attending to their meaning.
2. *Of the meaning,* concerning the analysis of the iconological factors that form the object, including style, taste, intentions, aspirations. It is the semantic aspect or the study of symbols, which includes the relationship between these symbols and what they denote.
3. *Of the function,* corresponding to the relationship between symbols and the issuers and recipients, in the pragmatic aspect.

These communicational levels can be related to the classical model of communication:

where:

- *Issuer*: the one who sends the message.
- *Mean*: channel through which the information flows.
- *Message*, the content of this information.
- *Code*, group of keys that make the information intelligible.
- *Reference*, cultural pattern in which the message acquires meaning.

- *Recipient*, the one who receives the information and decodes the message.

In regards to decoding, one must consider the problem created by the *noise* of which there has been previous mention; Bruno Munari understands noise as the set of filters that impede receiving the messages correctly or completely and result in the impossibility of answers or wrong answers.

Some of the noises that stand out are visual alterations of the environment, such as those of large cities where the messages are lost among the enormous amount of images that surround them.[57]

And so, according to Jakobson's original analysis applied by J. Llovet, the following representative scheme of the fundamental functions of semeiotics is created, where:

- *Emotional*: defines the relationships between the issuer and the message, because, by communicating he expresses a specific attitude in regards to the object of the communication, representing the affective and subjective part of the communication.
- *Phatic*: whose objective is to ensure contact among the subjects of the communicative process.
- *Poetical*: also called esthetical, concerning the message's plastic value.
- *Metalinguistic*: consists of the sense of the signs from another conceptual system.
- *Referential*: defines the relationships between the message and the object.
- *Connotative*: related to the relationships between the message and its recipient.

---

[57] Noises that just as abundant are sensorial noises (subjective disabilities to perceive colours); operative (obstacles from mental structures) and cultural (difficulties derived from the different cultural patterns to which the issuer and the receptor respond). Bruno Munari. *Design and Visual Communication*, p. 78

Both Llovet and Jakobson see the act of communication as "the construction, on behalf of an issuer, of a message that is coined based on the frame of articulatory possibilities of a linguistic code that is common to both the issuer and the recipient to whom the message is directed, transported through a channel and which is supposedly speaking of something contextual to which the message refers".[58]

In the theory of design, many attempts to apply this model specifically have been made but none of them has managed to provide new criteria that modify Llovet's model. This way, for example, there are those who identify the designer with the issuer and identify him based on a series of personal and social attributes with not much relevance. In relation to this subject, Daniel Prieto (*Design and communication*) can be consulted, among others.

Both the classical model of communication and its adaptation to design constitute a synthesis of its complexity which includes technical as well as objective, subjective and intersubjective factors that insert it into the social reality and explain why it cannot be alien to the industrial and commercial demands that make it susceptible to manifesting itself as part of the educational, advertising, electoral, ideological, religious, and even strictly aesthetic discourses.

Consequently, communication is inherent to design. Every design can be explained with the elements of the communicational process and every designer, whether or not he accepts or understands it, fulfils an expressive function contained in the information transmitted by the object.

The communicative role of design determines that it is not limited to the object's text but that it necessarily involves the context in which it is given and that the relationship formed between the object's text and context is what allows the emergence of specific contents of the object; its clarity and precision, therefore depend on the knowledge that the designer has of the social reality.

---

58 J. Llovet, *Op. cit.*, pgs. 94-96

The complexity of design is so much more tricky in that its language is not only verbal, but includes images, colours, shapes, sounds, symbols, etc., whose wide range demands, in addition to well-structured languages, among other conditions, informative accuracy, objectivity of the signs, univocal codification, absence of ambiguities, etc.

This is a general view of the characteristics on which design methodology is based; it is presented as a synthesis of the complexity that determines the designer's task to which the most important theoretic models in design make reference in one way or another.

DESIGN METHODS

Design Method: Bruno Munari

Bruno Munari, in *Art as a profession*, considers the designer to be a planner gifted with an aesthetic sense that he develops in different sectors: visual design, industrial design, graphic design and research design.

To design is to conceive a project, which is constituted by elements aiming at objectivity. Logic is its principle: if a problem is described logically, it will give rise to a structural logic, whose matter will be logical and, consequently, so will its form.

A well-made design results in the practice of the profession of design, where the beauty of that which is designed is there thanks to the coherent structure and the exactitude in the solving of its various components. Beauty, affirms Munari, "is the consequence of what is just"[59] and that is accomplished by letting the object form through its own means.

Currently, in the western world, the use of signs is more and more extended, the receiver lives surrounded by innumerable visual

[59] To understand Bruno Munari's grounds and method, read his texts *Art as a Profession, Design and Visual Communication,* and *How are Objects Born?*

stimuli, some of which remain in his conscience, while others remain as unconscious references. The great multitude of images corresponds to the so-called visual pollution, because they assault the user indiscriminately, there are no criteria of organization in the visual information.

Speaking of visual pollution carries a reflection regarding the teaching of design. The designer must learn, insists Munari (*Design and visual communication*), that he is an intentional informer and therefore must make it so that the meaning of his messages is completely received in them. The most important aspect of visual communication, according to this author, is the process of production of visual messages, which he places in a scheme of communication as follows:

The professional designer must determine the factors that visually alter the environment so that they are controllable in the message's expression, which at the same time is analyzed from two perspectives: information and visual support or group of elements that make the message visible.

In order to do so, the designer must have a method that will allow him to carry out his project with the adequate material, precise techniques and with the form that corresponds to its functions (including the psychological function).

Bruno Munari takes the fundaments of his first methodological model from the schemes of Archer, Fallon, Sidal and Asimow and based on them he designs constant guides to signalize actions to follow in order to reach the construction of the prototype, which is graphed like this:

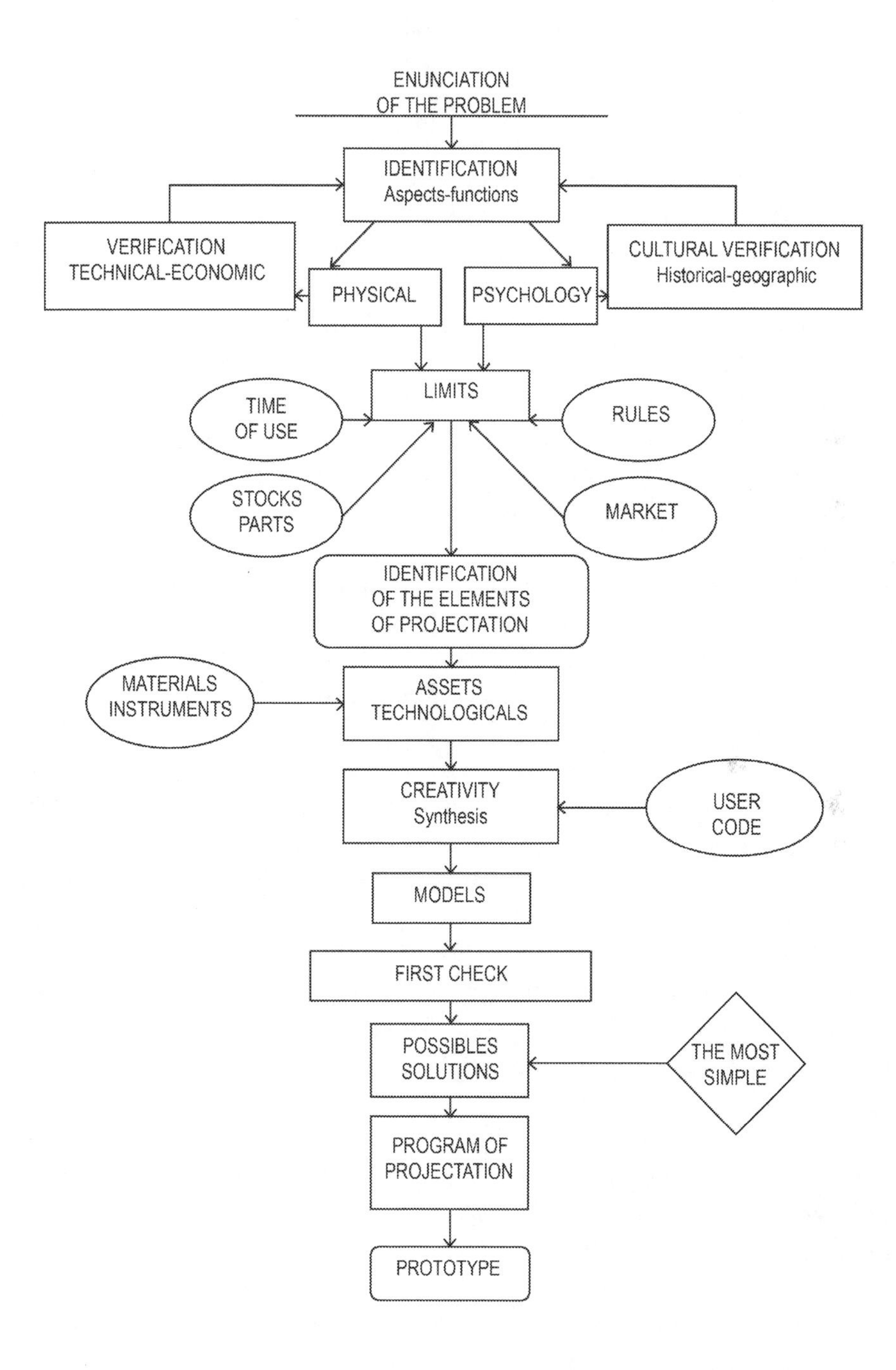
ENUNCIATION
OF THE PROBLEM
IDENTIFICATION
Aspects-functions
VERIFICATION
TECHNICAL-ECONOMIC
CULTURAL VERIFICATION
Historical-geographic
PHYSICAL
PSYCHOLOGY
LIMITS
TIME
OF USE
RULES
STOCKS
PARTS
MARKET
IDENTIFICATION
OF THE ELEMENTS
OF PROJECTATION
MATERIALS
INSTRUMENTS
ASSETS
TECHNOLOGICALS
CREATIVITY
Synthesis
USER
CODE
MODELS
FIRST CHECK
POSSIBLES
SOLUTIONS
THE MOST
SIMPLE
PROGRAM OF
PROJECTATION
PROTOTYPE

The author describes the model but in a way that he does not allow the reader to consider the factors of application of each of the so-called constants of the design method.

Munari does not consider his to be *the model*, as shown by *How objects are born?* where he proposes a new scheme. In this work, he reaffirms the priority of scheming in the task of design; he defines the design method as a series of necessary operations, arranged in a logical order that is dictated by experience. Its aim is to obtain a maximum result with the minimum effort... in the field of design, it is also wrong to design without a method, to think in an artistic manner looking to find an idea right away without conducting a previous study to obtain all the necessary information of what has already been made in the field of what is to be designed, without knowing what materials should be used to build something, without pinning down its exact function.

The method –continues this author-, is an applicable instrument that mustn't under any circumstances be considered as absolute and definite; it is, therefore, modifiable if during the development of the practice for the method's application, there were other objective values that improve the process.

Munari distinguishes the professional designer, who owns a model with which he develops with more certainty his task of romantic designer, who prefers brainstorms that force the technique to develop contingent and arbitrary elements.

As in the previous scheme, Munari begins with the problem, because it considers it to have all the elements for its solution; therefore, first one must define the problem as a whole and the type of solution that is sought.

Every problem is susceptible to being broken down into small particular problems that can be solved partially, turning to, if that were the case, previous solutions provided by other researchers.

Munari's new model recognizes oriental influences and is described compared with a green rice recipe, as follows:

The comparison is polemic in that it contributes to the conception of design methodology as a group of recipes that solve all design-related problems that the professional might face, impairing their character of support tools.

As an assistant to the model of design, Munari proposes an analysis index card of the existing objects in order to understand them with all the possible aspects and target values such as:

- *Object name*, must be appropriate.
- *Author*, whose knowledge allows in some cases, determining the design method.
- *Producer.*
- *Dimensions*, because the good performance depends on the mobility, which depends on adequate dimensions.
- *Material*, appropriate in regards to its function.
- *Weight*, with regards to the dimensions.
- *Techniques*, as forms of work of the material.
- *Cost*, to purchase it at the sae price as other similar objects that perform similar functions.
- *Packaging*, type, information, protection, etc.
- *Declared utility.*
- *Functionality*, of the parts and their relationship with the effort.
- *Noise*, whether the object has mechanical or motive parts.
- *Maintenance*, whether she object requires it and how it is conducted or if it needs special protection.
- *Ergonomics*, consisting of the object's relationship with the activities that man developed to use it.
- *Finish*, such as resistance, texture, etc.
- *Mobility* for its transferring or moving.
- *Duration* or period of operation and the particular environmental changes that it produces.
- *Toxicity*, determined in relation to the user.
- *Aesthetics*, related to the coherent mode like the parts that form the whole.
- *Fashion, styling*, whether the object represents specific symbols of wellbeing, luxury or class (though it must be known these actually are not objects of design).

- *Social value*, according to the functions performed by the object: work division, cultural or technological contributions to the community, etc.
- *Essentiality*, to determine whether the object has more elements than necessary.
- *Precedents*, knowing them may help indicate whether it has suffered a logical evolution.
- *Acceptance by the public*, linked to rejection of advertising.

Integrated Generalizing Design

Victor Papanek

Design "is the conscious effort to impose a meaningful order",[60] affirms Victor Papanek when describing this discipline as a conscious intention to solve problems, whose organization will dictate the exactitude of their answers.

To achieve functionality as well as significance, the author proposes the development of the function complex. The diagram shows the interacting dynamic of the elements that should be considered in design, which are described next:

- *Method*, interaction of tools, treatments and materials, which will be used optimally, economically and efficiently.
- *Use*, must respond adequately to the question: is it useful?
- *Need*, not referring to passing or superfluous desires, but to true economic, psychological, spiritual, technologic and intellectual demands, that are harder to meet than those carefully manipulated demands implanted by fashion or novelty.
- *Telesis*, reflection of the conditions that give way to a design, so that it will adapt to the socioeconomic order in which it will act, avoiding anachronism or yearning for old times which create consumerism.

---

60 Victor Papanek develops these concepts in his work *Design for the Real World*.

- *Association,* psychological condition that predisposes sympathy or empathy to a given value.
- *Aesthetics,* configuration of forms and colours that results in meaningful entities that move or gratify by stimulating the senses.

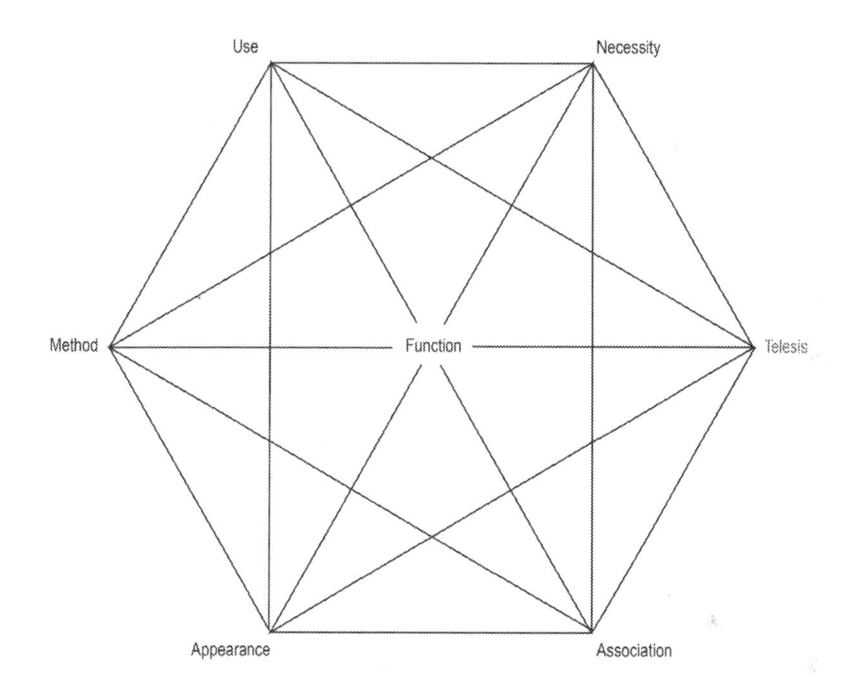

The complex's elements are related thanks to the function, to the way in which the design fulfils its purpose, consisting in transforming man's environment and tools, and therefore, man himself.

Transforming the social environment involves considering the human being's location as limitations: the environment in which he lives, the skill that allows him to live and the certainty of his mortality. The triad of limitations is useful as a primary filter to establish the social value of the act of design, directly linked to the hexalateral function complex.

In regards to social responsibility, it is understood as the reflection concerning the large sectors of population that are discriminated by a design that seems to be destined to a public that is limited to the ideal consumer (age: between 18 and 25 years old; height: 1.80 m 'exactly'; weight: 80 kg 'exactly'; gender male, race white and middle income).

Constant diversity is added to the ideal consumer in a single object, and so the user who wishes to acquire a chair finds himself having to choose among 21,336 different models, among which there are probably 500 good ones, and only some – three according to Papanek - that fulfil the requirements of low price, functionality, maintenance, storage, transportation, disregard for social conditioning, etc.

The design process – continues Papanek – must join three steps: the description of the need to solve a problem, the definition of that aspect of behaviour of problem solving – called 'created' -, and the suggestion of some methods that allow for the problems solving.

In *Designer for the Real World*, Papanek proposes both pedagogic as well as methodological alternatives in design. In regards to the pedagogical aspect, he emphasizes the multidisciplinary relationship with which becoming familiar with other specialties is an important point for the design student to develop his capacity to acknowledge, isolate, define and solve problems. The multidisciplinary aspect supports the association capacity and enriches the magnitude of knowledge and the memory's quality. This is indispensable for design in the skill of considering things from new viewpoints.

> [...] even the moment of going to school for the first time, it seems like everybody has the capacity to solve practically identical problems. And so sensorial, cultural or associational-type obstacles begin to form, which inhibit the creative capacity that is inherent to the person.

The ability to solve problems in new and unexpected ways is obstructed and the design student requires new methods that will allow him to develop design based on alternative reason guidelines from which different approaches will result; the student and the professional must give themselves the chance to experiment as well as to fail developing an obliged sense of responsibility by both.

In design schools students learn how to dominate the object or image; there, the designer alters, modifies, eliminates or produces design standards, but mastery is assumed in the demythologizing of the philosophy with which designers nowadays act based on five myths:

that of production in series, that of falling into abeyance, that of 'what the people want', that of the designer's lack of command, and that of 'quality no longer counts'.

The student must graduate aware that he has more control over his work than he thinks, especially because he will design for a small local market and not for most of the people in the world.

Victor Papanek's method is derived from the pedagogical aspect and insists on the interdisciplinary teams in which related specialities allow the designer to broaden the spectra of innovative creative penetration.

In design, the link between man and his environment gives way to the *integrated generalizing design* as an approach to a process that considers both the form and the function that are inserted in a unified and susceptible vital medium of growth, change, mutation, adaptation and regeneration as answers to man's needs.

Integrated design is not a group of skills, techniques or mechanical processes, but involves a careful analysis of the problems, whose complexity assumes a historical perspective, specific factors, human, biological and social perspectives. The tendency of design schools is to form close-minded, 'vertical' specialists, when what we need are generalizers or 'horizontal' synthesizers, open minded.

The integrated generalizing method is based on considering the problem of design either as a specific case or as a general issue where what matters is the functional treatment of the idea and the comprehension of the procedure and its connections with analogous procedures. The author gives the following example:

A *specific case*: 'design a chair', the student will start with the general concept 'chair', he will revise design strategies, and based on these strategies he will develop a series of apparent 'groups' or possibilities to solve the problem. He will choose from the general case his particular group and continue until reaching the solution of his own specific case.

- *A:* 'Phase' of design. From the specific case to the general case, and from there to the specific case. And a *general case:*

'design something to help underdeveloped countries'; here, the student devotes an extensive research of different sources and disciplines based on which he reaches the specific-case concept 'source of energy similar to the bicycle'. The concept's development will meet multiple prolongations and will lead to different solutions for the general case (this type of problems is rarely raised in the schools).

- *B:* 'Phase' of design. From the general case to the specific case and to the general case (team problem). A and B can be considered shackles of continuous cyclic chains.
- *C:* Series of 'phases' of design cyclic character
- *D:* Linking of 'phases' of design (one cycle)
- *E:* Multidirectional network of several 'phases of design
- *F:* Schematic representations of the behaviour of a multidisciplinary team. Only a small portion of the hexagonal network is shown

A series of possible 'phases' of design (A and B) will produce a multidirectional and bidirectional network of equilateral triangles arranged, without wasting space, so that they form adjoining hexagons.

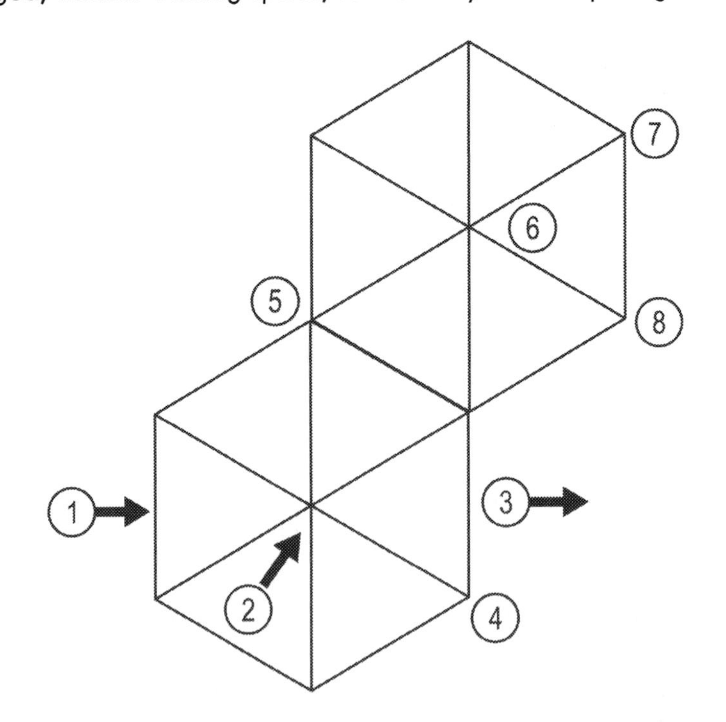

In order to understand all the branches of integrated generalizing design it is indispensable to review all the parameters that are related to the design process through the elaboration of an organization chart, which works in a simple manner if the interconnections are clear. It is important that it be read in one browse and, by definition, it is never completed, leaving open the possibility of indefinitely adding concepts and new categories and, thus, new connections.

Once the phases are comprehended, it is possible to establish the successive stages through which every work of design passes:

- Formation of a design team that is representative of all the relevant disciplines, as well as components of the 'client' group.
- Establishment of primary organization chart.
- Research and inquiry phase.
- Conclusion of the first half of the organization chart.
- Establishment of the second half of the organization chart: what to do?
- Individual design, or in pairs, or in team, and development of ideas.
- Confrontation of these designs with the goals proposed in the organization chart and correction of design and organization chart in light of the design experiences.
- Construction of models, prototypes, test models and work models.
- Testing of the models by the relevant group-user.
- Incorporation of the results of these tests into the organization chart.
- Final design and verification, and conclusion of the design along with any written reports, graphic communications.
- Employment of organization chart as a verification guide of the characteristics of the objects of design and guide in future design works of similar nature.

Papanek explains that the reality of the design process can never follow such a rectilinear and sequential path as the list suggests. The follow-up of design demands a constant dynamic of the methods for the solving of problems and, mostly, integrated design requires flexibility; therefore, the author proposes the triangles and their joining in a hexagonal piece that allows playing, as with a puzzle, forming the more appropriate structure. According to the author's opinion, there is no other way of representing the phases' simultaneity character.

What is most important, insists Papanek, is that design be responsible toward the environment, that is accomplish maximum requiring minimum, that it consume only what is necessary, that it use things for longer periods of time, in so many words, that it be revolutionary and radical.

Input-output relationship

Christopher Jones

Christopher Jones, in *Design Methods* considers that the designer elaborates a chain of interrelated specifications and predictions to formulate proposals that respond to the given requirements. The method is the means to solve the conflict "between rational analysis and creative thought".[61]

The method transcends because it exteriorizes the design process in a diagram of symbols that represent the process's phases and relationships. The designer uses this model from three perspectives: creativity, rationality and organized control of the process; thus making it explainable, in a way that the decisions in design acquire a coherent and conscious meaning.

The design method modifies the traditional ways of confronting complex problems. The obstacles that the modern designer faces surpass the traditional complexity and are manifested out of the reach of simple processes.

Christopher Jones explains the *perspectives of design methodology*:

- *From the creative viewpoint*, the designer is a black box out of which comes a mysterious creative leap.

---

[61] In *Design Methods,* Christopher Jones presents the relational tables between the input and output methods

- *From the rational viewpoint*, the designer is a glass box inside which can be discerned a completely explicable rational process.
- *From the control viewpoint,* the designer is a self organizing system capable of finding shortcuts across unknown territory. This last viewpoint is the only one that leads directly to the practical value of design theory.

According to this author's opinion, the designer effectively controls the process of answers or *outputs* in which he trusts and of which no completely rational explanation can be expected, because – affirms Jones – they refer directly to variations that occur in the brain due to the infinite number of stimuli or *inputs* received from the outside. According to this, the memory assimilates immediate or distant experiences and models them in the memory.

The cerebral process of forming ideas is nonlinear; it advances, moves back or feeds back the different experiences passing mainly through three stages: *divergence*, as an amplification of situational limits; *transformation*, as a critical stage; and *convergence* in which a gamut of options is reduced to a single possibility.

In design, divergence, transformation and convergence are three moments in the method in which *inputs-outputs* or stimuli-answers are managed, based on that, Jones proposes a different confrontation with complex problems.

According to the author, a complicated problem must be turned into a simple one through the stratification of elements, based on a precise mental picture that exposes the crucial aspects of the problem. For that, Jones presents a synthetic chart of symbolic strategies, suitable especially for solving the systems' needs whose hierarchic treatment is important.

Jones considers that "methodology should not be a fixed track to a fixed destination, but a conversation about everything that could be made to happen", therefore, he proposes a table of methodological alternatives in the crossings between *inputs* and *outputs*, whose complexity surpasses the limits of this work, and so, by way of illustration, only two charts are annexed, that of stages and methods selection, and the *inputs-outputs* table, whose thorough comprehension demands consulting the proposed bibliography.

GUIDE-TABLE FOR THE SELECTION OF DESIGN METHODS

SELECTION OF DESIGN METHODS

1. Decide which of the table's *inputs* is already known.
2. Choose, from among the *outputs*, the information category that is required.
3. In the squares in which the chosen *output* files and columns intersect, appear methods that are appropriate for solving the problem; for example, method 5.3 AIDA is in file 4 of input and column 5 of output. Following are the methods arranged as they appear in the book.

INPUT-OUTPUT TABLE FOR CHOOSING DESIGN METHODS

SELECTION OF METHODS OF DESING

1. Choose which one of the inputs of the table is already known.
2. Select, between the outputs, the category of information that is required.
3. In the boxes where the rows and columns of the chosen outputs cross the proper methods appear for the solution of the problem; for example., the method 5.3 AIDA is in the row 4 of input. The methods have been annotated below by their order of appearence in the book.

1:PREFABRICATED STRATEGIES (CONVERGENCE)

1.1 Systematic investigation (Aprox. of the theory of the decisions)
1.2 Analisis of values
1.3 Systems Engineering
1.4 Design of the system man-machine
1.5 Investigation of the limits
1.6 Acumulative strategy of Page
1.7 CASA (Collaborative Strategy for Adaptable Architecture)

2: CONTROL OF STRATEGIES

2.1 Change of strategy
2.2 Fundamental method of design of Matchett (M.F.D.)

3: METHODS OF EXPLORATION OF SITUATIONS OF DESIGN (DIVERGENCE)

3.1 Definition of objectives
3.2 Investigation of the literature
3.3 Investigation of the visual inconsistency
3.4 Interviews with the user
3.5 Questionnaires
3.6 Investigation of the behavior of the user
3.7 Systematic essays
3.8 Selection of scales of measurement
3.9 Registry and reduction of data

4:METHODS OF INVESTIGATION OF IDEAS (DIVERGENCES AND TRANSFORMATION)

4.1 Brainstorming
4.2 Synesthesia
4.3 Disappearance of mental block
4.4 Morphological diagram

5: METHODS OF EXPLORATION OF THE STRUC-TURE OF THE PROBLEM (TRANSFORMATION)

5.1 Matrix of interactions
5.2 Network of interactions
5.3 AIDA (Analysis of Interconnected Decision Areas)
5.4 Transfromation of the system
5.5 Innovation by change of limits
5.6 Functional Innovation
5.7 Method of determination of components of Alexander
5.8 Classification of the information of desing

6: METHODS OF EVALUATION CONVERGENCE

6.1 List of data
6.2 Criteria of selection
6.3 Classification and consideration
6.4 Written specifications
6.5 Index of suitability of Quirk

Table input-output for the selection de methods of design

OUTPUTS → INPUTS ↓	**2** **Explored situation of design**	**3** **Perceived or transformed structure of the problem**	**4** **Localized limits, described subsolutions and Identified Conflicts**	**5** **Combined Subsolutions in alternative designs**	**6** **Valuated alternative designs and final design chosen**
1 **Transmited order**	3.1 Definition of objectives 3.2 Investigation of the literature 3.3 Investigation of the visual inconsistency 3.4 Interviews with the user 4.1 Brainstorming	3.2 Investigation of the literature 3.3 Investigation of the visual inconsistency 3.4 Interviews with the user 4.1 Brainstorming 4.2 Synesthesia	3.3 Investigation of the visual inconsistency 4.1 Brainstorming 4.4 Morphological diagram	3.3 Investigation of the visual inconsistency 4.1 Brainstorming 4.2 Synesthesia	2.1 Change of strategy 2.2 Fundamental method of design of Matchett (M.F.D.)
2 **Explored situation of design**		3.1 Definition of objectives 3.9 Registry and reduction of data 5.1 Matrix of interactions 5.2 Network of interactions 5.8 Classification of the information of desing 6.4 Written specifications		5.4 Transfromation of the system 5.6 Functional innovation 5.7 Method of determination of components of Alexander	
3 **Perceived or transformed structure of the problem**	3.2 Investigation of the literature 3.5 Questionnaires 3.6 Investigation of the behavior of the user 3.7 Systematic essays 3.8 Selection of scales of measurement 3.9 Registry and reduction of data		1.5 Investigation of the limits 3.7 Systematic essays 4.1 Brainstorming 4.4 Morphological diagram 6.2 Criteria of selection 6.3 Classification and consideration 6.4 Written specifications	4.1 Brainstorming 4.2 Sinestesia 5.4 Transfromation of the system 5.5 Innovation by change of limits	1.1 Systematic investigation 1.2 Analisis of values 1.3 Systems Engineering 1.4 Design of the system man-machine 1.5 Investigation of the limits 1.6 Acumulative strategy of Page 1.7 CASA
4 **Localized limits, described subsolutions and Identified Conflicts**		4.1 Brainstorming 4.3 Disappearance of mental block 5.3 AIDA 5.4 Transfromation of the system 5.5 Innovation by change of limits 5.6 Functional Innovation 5.7 Method of determination of components of Alexander		4.1 Brainstorming 4.2 Synesthesia 4.3 Disappeerance of mental block 5.3 AIDA	5.3 AIDA
5 **Combined Subsolutions in alternative designs**					1.2 Analisis of values 3.5 Questionnaires 3.6 Investigation of the behavior of the user 3.7 Systematic essays 3.8 Selection of scales of measurement 3.9 Registry and reduction of data 6.1 List of data 6.2 Criteria of selection 6.3 Classification and consideration 6.4 Written specifications 6.5 Index of suitability of Quirk
6 **Valuated alternative designs and final design chosen**					

Creative process of problem solving

Bernd Löbach

Bernd Löbach considers the design process to be a set of possible relationships between the designer and the designed object, so that it will be a technologically reproducible product.

For the process to work, the designer as a producer of ideas must collect different pieces of information with which he works to solve a design problem, where creative capabilities are indispensable for choosing the right data and applying it to relevant situations.

The way of manifesting the creative aspect is the establishment of novel relationships based on previous knowledge and experiences that are linked to the specific information of a given problem. The amount of possible combinations and the probability of different solutions are derived from a multidimensional tackling of the problem.

This way, the design process involves both the creative aspects and the problem-solving procedures that remain constant:

- A problem exists and is exposed.
- Data regarding the problem is gathered, valued and related creatively.
- Solutions for the problem are developed and judged according to established criteria.
- The most adequate solution is conducted.[62]

What's important is the designer's effort in each of the phases to define and focus on the solution: a design object whose use will cover needs in a long-lasting fashion.

Löbach expresses the stages of the design process in the following model.

---

[62] Bernd Löbach explores in depth his conception on design methodology in his text *Industrial Design*

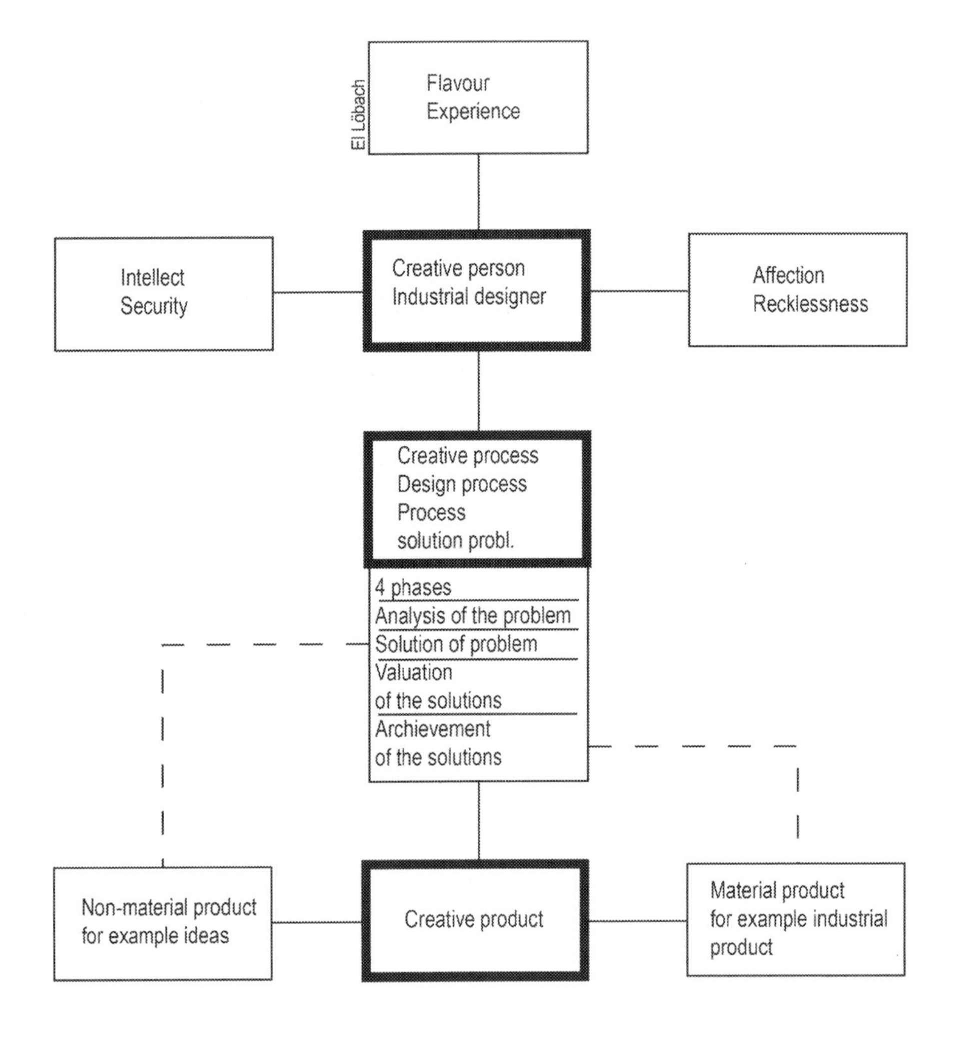
El Löbach
Flavour
Experience
Intellect
Security
Creative person
Industrial designer
Affection
Recklessness
Creative process
Design process
Process
solution probl.
4 phases
Analysis of the problem
Solution of problem
Valuation
of the solutions
Archievement
of the solutions
Non-material product
for example ideas
Creative product
Material product
for example industrial
product

It is the author's opinion that the stages are developed in a much more complex way than that expressed in the model, because each moment is not delimited by its real course, it always entwines with others and its movement involves both advances as well as regressions.

To explain the four stages, Löbach presents in the following chart the breakdown of actions that must be performed by the designer:

Stage 1: Problem analysis

The starting point is detecting the problem, whose raising, according to Löbach, is actually generally presented to the designer by the company.

In order to analyze the problem, with the intention of coming up with the best solution, it is indispensable to compile all the data concerning it. Here, any information contributes to the foundation over which an answer will be constructed. Löbach breaks down the possibilities:

- The *need analysis* studies how many people are interested in the problem's solution.
- The *social relationship analysis* refers to the link between a probable user and the object, considering its extended description.
- The *analysis of relations with the surroundings* considers the environment in which the object will be inserted. The special circumstances to which the object will be exposed and the environment's possible actions (meteorological conditions, soiling, etc), are studied, and vice versa (environmental overload, contamination, etc).
- The *historical development analysis* considers the evolution of the object's design.
- The *market analysis* includes data on similar objects and their behaviour in order to obtain common points of reference. It is also considered as a comparative analysis of the product.
- The *function analysis* includes technical data regarding the object's use. Here, an object's characteristics are structured according to its functional qualities; the system of representation is the so-called 'topographic tree'.
- The *structural analysis* reveals the object's components and its relationships, based on which decisions are made regarding the object's so-called technological maturity.

- The *configuration analysis* specifies the object's points of aesthetical appearance. The formal characteristics and their possible variants are established.
- The *analysis of materials and manufacturing processes* considers the means.
- The *risk analysis* considers patents, determinations and standards that could affect the problem's solving.
- The *system analysis* determines the object's relations with the group to which it belongs, if that were the case.
- The *distribution elements analysis* reviews aspects such as assembling, customer service and maintenance.

The problem's definition is expressed verbally and visually, based on that, the factors that intervene in the solution are valued and classified.

Stage 2: Problem solutions

Based on associations between the information and the conclusion regarding conditions for the problem solving, the designer incursions into the creative stage. In that stage, he chooses procedures for the organized solution (*trial, error and inspiration*).

The elaboration of ideas involves defining different possibilities for solving the problem at issue, it is fundamental that sketches be made or model built to test the thought-out solutions.

Stage 3: Evaluation of problem solutions

This stage includes the thorough testing of the presented alternatives, among which the designer chooses that which responds to a careful confrontation with the necessary values that are set as conclusions to stage 1. The evaluation procedures are not described in the text but are indeed related to two dimensions: the importance that the new object has for the user and its importance for the company.

Stage 4: Realization of the problem solution

In this stage, an answer is specified and the smallest details are completed with the necessary drawings graphic explanations.

Creative process	=Proceso of solution to the problem	- Process of design (development of the product)
1. Phase of preparation	Analysis of the problem Knowledge of the problem Storing of information, scientific valuation	Analysis of the design problem Analysis of the necessity Analysis of the social relation (man-product) Analysis of the relation with the surroundings (product-surroundings) Historical development Analysis of the market/analysis of the product Analysis of the function (practical functions) Structural analysis (constructive structure) Analysis of configuration (aesthetic functions) Analysis of materials and manufacture, Patents, prescriptions, norms System analysis of products (product-product) Distribution, assembly, service to custumers, maintenance
	Definition of the problem, classification of the problem, definition of objectives	Fixation of valuations Exigencies for the new product
2. Phase of incubation	Solutions to the problem Election of methods to solve the problem, production of ideas, solutions of the problem	Solutions of design Concept of design Solutions of principle Schemes of ideas Scale models or models Valuation of the design solutions
3. Phase of illumination	Valuation of the solutions to the problem Examination of solutions, process of selection, process of valuation	Election of the best solution Connection with the conditions in new product
4. Phase of verification	Realization of the solution of the problem Realization of the solution of the problem, repeated valuation of the solution	Solution of design Construction Structural constitution Configuration of the details (elements on watch) Development of models Drawings Documentation

Method / Taxonomy

Abraham Moles

Abraham Moles does not propose, as other authors do, a model of design method; he limits himself to providing a series of analytical charts indicating the objects, which constitute the fundamental constant of his work. He affirms that the close relationship of man with his objects is manifested through the placing of these objects in closed spaces that are identified with a determined functionality in the arrangement.

The common denominator is the arrangement that is directly linked to the semantic distance and the problem of density: a space for each object, where it occupies the volume that is offered to it.

An object intervenes in the prolongation of the human act as well as in the systematization of sensible elements, this way it acts as mediator between every man and society.

To speak of culture –affirms Moles– involves an inescapable reference to the artificial environment, man organizes the surroundings and places the objects in defined access spheres, each one of which means a particular a particular and comprehensible dominion. This way it is man who created the so-called *relational set*.

Moles establishes a pertinent distinction between things (referring only to natural systems, separable and enunciable) and objects (elements that are really of human creation); for him,

> [...] everyday life introduces the sociological dimension in what is immediately lived, above all through the transformation of objects into goods, into subjects of desire with a function of carriers of signs and social exponents, with opposition between private and public, between artificial and natural.[63]

---

[63] *Theory of Objects* is the work in which Abraham Moles presents his taxonomy of objects and his methodological models

Moles bases his procedure in the appreciation that, if there is a universe of objects with its own epistemological dimensions, then it responds to an order that would be interesting to know, and he does so with integrated classifications in what he calls *taxonomic method.*

First, he established categories: the object itself; isolated object; object located in contexts; objects in groups: interrelated group; objects on a large-scale: a group devoid of mutual relationship property. The development of taxonomy does not care for the so-called 'isolated piece' because it is reabsorbed at some point and inserted within a context.

To classify, he uses the concept of organizing distance or semantic distance, by way of which the individual places pairs of objects that are interrelated on a scale of coherent distances and spaces.

The most basic relationships are assumed in the so-called life of the *object-individual* couple, whose stages are:

1. *Wanting the object*, this may be in the form of: prolonged desire that grows with time, need or permanent and constant function, and impulsive desire as a passing gesture that weakens through oblivion.
2. *Acquisition* or the object's passing from a collective universe to the personal sphere where the maximum pleasure occurs at the moment of purchase.
3. *Discovering the object,* understood as cognitive comprehension.
4. *Love of the object*, a progressive discovery of virtues and defects, and the object's approach to its idealized image.
5. *Object habit.* Once it is explored, it goes on to form part of the surrounding world; it is neutral and returns to existence according to its use.
6. *Object upkeep.* The object returns to existence as soon as it is repaired.
7. *Object death.* The individual indices the object and replaces it.

The second relationship involves that which includes with which is included, that which is taken in and that in which we penetrate; here, Moles locates four scopes: objects in which one penetrates; objects of our size and with scarce mobility; objects sustained by the former or contained in them; and micro-objects that are held between fingers.

Based on this differentiation he establishes the so-called hunting preserves or spheres of access to objects. These are determined spaces in which the collection of objects is located; they form the limits of the object universe of an individual and, in them the objects' maximum density is located.

The types of spheres are: the shell of immediate gesture; the personal empire (house-room); the functional empire (work space); the distribution empires (stores); the reserves (warehouses, non-public spaces); intermediate reserve circuits (antiquary and attic); public reserve and exhibition circuits (museums, galleries, etc.).

In these hunting preserves, the individual distributes, acquires or evacuate the objects. The classification is determined by factors such as function, traditions, or their direct link to super-functions such as eating, sleeping, resting, etc. This way, centres of interest are created which condition the objects' functional division.

Classifying involves the possibility of meeting the objects again, according to variables such as social function, social position, individual strengths or negative forces of money or time.

The classification results in the following forms in which man relates to the objects in the described hunting preserves:

- *Ascetic:* objects are dangerous enemies from which a distance must be kept; distrust the attraction that they exert on the individuals.
- *Hedonistic:* the possession of objects entails pleasure and the aim is to increase it.
- *Aggressive:* hunting, destroying, it is taking possession of the object without becoming alienated (although the aggressive act also alienates).
- *Acquisition:* the most common, turns man into a coextensive system of his possessions: things are the extension of man.

- *Aesthetic:* based on the social concept of pure beauty, motor of the art lover; it is an acquisitive manner but without the accumulation criterion.
- *Surrealist:* based on the external relationship the disposition of objects and forms, in the juxtaposition of rare elements, a characteristic of *gadgets*.
- *Functionalist*: the objects exist exclusively from their role, which places them in the conscience that postulates eventual absence of alienation and rigor of thought.
- *Kitsch*: a compound linked to acquisitiveness, hedonistic pleasure of possession, pseudo-functionalist; global consumption in which accumulation and multiplicity are essential.

Starting with the object's study, based on his classifications, he elaborates a statistical phenomenology that involves an approach to society's development and to the individual's place in that society.

A description of objects held in specific places speaks of the frame of daily life, determined by the theory of needs; the amount, variety and types of object collections reflect the development of industrial civilization.

The taxonomic method facilitates closeness to the objects' language, which always contains – in the words of Abraham Moles– two aspects: semantic (denotative) freely explicable by the receiver, and aesthetic (connotative), built over the sense's harmonics, over the degrees of freedom that the standard of pure meaning leaves to variations, the meaning of an object, its semantics is linked to a great extent to its function. This position differs from other semiotic methods –like that of Roland Barthes– for which the semantic aspect is the connotative one.

The designer can benefit from applying the taxonomic method because it allows him to organize the objects' structure rationally and objectively according to both the user and the market.

This taxonomy facilitates an analysis of the functions that are attributed to the object, in general and in partial aspects such as handicraft, durability, cleaning, etc. The following chart is an example:

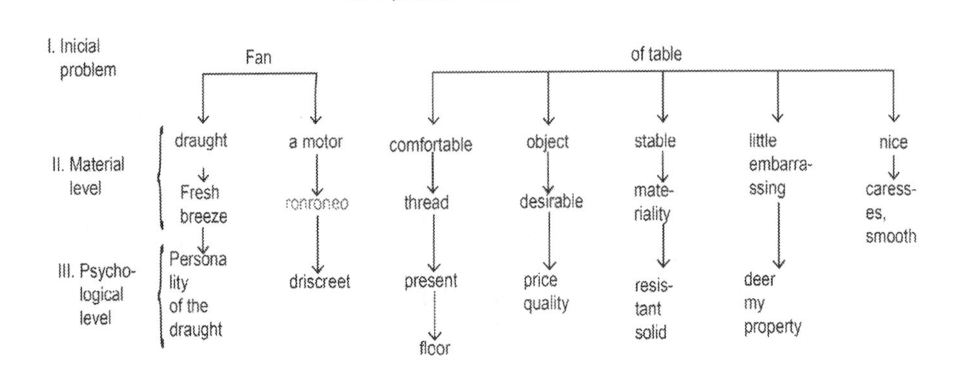

Here is a list of demands pertinent to an object like the table ventilator to which we have attributed global functions in the previous chart. Rational design attempts to obtain, in relation to the object's functions, a group decomposition of the functional demands, characterizing them as elemental functions either in a positive (small, big) or negative way (too small, too big, too lightweight, etc). These functions are regrouped into super-functions related to dimensions, weight, safety, longevity, aspect, etc., which at the same time are regrouped into very general descriptive families (geometrical description, role, aspect, sale, relation with other objects) that can be found a little everywhere, whichever the analyzed object. The structure constituted this way supposes a first determination of what is desired in regards to the object, which may constitute the articles and conditions of design.

List of exigencies (soll wert)

	Superfunciones	Elementary functions	
Geometric Description	Global dimensions	▶ too small	1
		▶ too big	2
	Global weight	▶ too light	3
		▶ too heavy	4
		shock ▶ deterioration ▶ false maneuver	5
	Security (nondangerous)	▶ danger ▶ security of use	6
		▶ protection	7
	Stability	▶ foot-polygon sustenation (own space)	8
		▶ forms (height)	9
Paper	Basic function subject	▶ weight	10
		▶ direction	11
		▶ volume	12
		▶ temperature	13
	Own	▶ movable component	14
		▶ cárter	15
		▶ dust	16
		▶ heating	17
	Longevity	▶ resistance	18
		▶ maintenance	19
Aspect	Pure function	▶ air volume	20
		▶ ornamentation	21
		▶ stainless	22
	Finished	▶ shining/mate	23
Sale (relation producer constumer)	Functionality of manufacture	▶ price/quality	24
		▶ investigation	25
		▶ some prices of materials	26
		▶ sum of operations that integrate it realization	27
	Functionality of maintenance	▶ easy disassembling	28
		▶ abarcable	29
		▶ easy substitution of pieces	30
		▶ forms	31
	Function of packing and presentation	▶ hanging parts (envelope simple)	32
		▶ caress smooth surfaces	33
		▶ size box/object	34
Relation with other objects	Function of relation	▶ property to a family	35
		▶ relations with the decoration	36
		▶ discreet color	37
		▶ price of market	38

This is just a conclusive example by Moles, since the management of taxonomy involves a broad study of his theory of objects; it also requires a direct relationship with semiotics to understand what this methodological alternative is based on. The major difficulty of the taxonomical method is the absence of a model that allows for the abstract comprehension of the procedure sequence and its direct application by designers.

Design Method

Gui Bonsiepe

Every design is based on the search for relevant information that will be useful for the decision-making process involved in problem solving. Understanding design as a decision-making process involves the identification of adequate criteria that will help guide the designer-researcher through the most relevant actions.

Designing also includes the rational reach, whose objective is to avoid an erratic behaviour and "to explain why a project has reached certain solutions and not others [...] based on some arguments".[64]

Planning means enumerating activities that contribute to a project's development, that simultaneously determine its sequence and content. This constitutes the methodological advice, whose usefulness lies in the coherent accessibility to the problems.

The methodological aspect, says Gui Bonsiepe, contributes to the breaking down of complexity in design, dividing a problem into ranked sub-problems. This scientific approach to design acquires its validity in that it is capable of organizing the knowledge that makes possible a tangible effect in the stages of design. A proper organization allows

---

64 To explore this method in depth, read the text by Gui Bonsiepe: *Industrial Design, Technology and Dependence*

capturing objectively and not intuitively the nature of the design process.

Bonsiepe uses the concept of *projecting* as a synonym of *designing*, although with other connotations, as he himself affirms; what's important is that both activities belong to a similar behaviour: problem-solving, where the results of projection or design are manifested in the product.

A design problem puts the designer in a stimulating but conflictive position, which in addition to provoking curiosity of knowledge, compels the desire for a result that cannot be solved in an immediate thought. To this, the apparently objective and neutral methods of design contribute.

Gui Bonsiepe defines methodology as a guide for the *problem-solver* in a specific *problem-solving* field, which helps to determine the sequence, content and specific procedures of the actions.

Before specifying his method, Bonsiepe contributes a typology of problems based on their definition (well-defined when the variables are closed, ill-defined or structured when they are open), this classification is displayed in general classes:

- Well-defined initial state and ill-defined terminal state.
- Well-defined initial state and well-defined terminal state.
- Ill-defined initial state and ill-defined final state.

Bonsiepe affirms that the most common mistake in methods is that the macrostructure (initial stages through which the designer passes in order to solve a design problem) is well exposed and defined, whereas the microstructure (detailed task in each of the different stages) is a mysterious element.

Based on the previous, this author defines what he considers are stages of the process of design:

1. *Problem structure*
2. *Design*
3. *Realization*

He subdivides each stage as followed:

1.1 *Operation: localization of a need.*
Technique (how to): search for a situation of disarrangement in the population or in the environment for which the design product is destined.

1.2 *Operation: evaluation of need.*
Technique: compare the need with others, in regards to compatibility and priority.

1.3 *Operation: design problem analysis in relation to its justification.*
Technique: it may occur that a design problem is false or unjustified. Comparing the function of the product that is to be designed with the proposal made by the sponsor, eventually erroneous approaches are discovered.

1.4 *Operation: definition of the design problem in general terms.*
Technique: based on recompiled background information, the project's general objectives and function are described.

1.5 *Operation: pinning down the design problem.*
Technique: the products specific requirements and subsystems are established. The controllable and non-controllable restrictions are formulated by the designer. The open variables are transformed, to the extent possible, into closed ones.

1.6 *Operation: problem subdivision into sub-problems.*
Technique: search for problems that are relatively independent among each other. Establish a division of functions.

1.7 *Operation: sub-problem ranking.*
Technique: search for key or neuralgic functions. Establish a matrix of interaction among sub-systems. Analyze their mutual dependence.

1.8 *Operation: analysis of existing solutions.*
Technique: compare solutions according to their advantages and disadvantages. Establish a typology of existing solutions. Evaluate the, according to a list of criteria, for example: complexity, costs, manufacturing, safety, precision, feasibility, technique, dependability.

2.1 *Operation: development of alternatives or basic ideas.*
Technique: "brainstorming", synectics, morphological analysis (Zwicky box). Visualization of these ideas through sketches, schemes, models (that is, qualitative and non-discursive codes).

2.2 *Operation: testing of alternatives.*
Technique: submit each proposal to testing of technical, functional, economical and form feasibility, compare advantages and disadvantages. For this aim, provisional models are elaborated, which simulate the details of the product in question.
2.3 *Operation: selection of the best alternatives.*
Technique: assign qualification values to a list of parameters, for example, complexity, safety, dependability, form coherence, costs rage, standards, simplicity of manufacturing, life span. Choose the alternative/s that scored highest.
2.4 *Operation: detail the chosen alternative.*
Technique: measure pieces; determine manufacturing processes and materials, tolerances, terminations. Prepare technical drafts for the manufacturing of the partial or total prototype.
2.5 *Operation: prototype construction.*
2.6 *Operation: prototype evaluation.*
Technique: observation of total product's behaviour.
2.7 *Operation: introduce eventual modifications.*
Technique: based on the testing of the provisional product, redesign or perfect the necessary details (that resulted deficient).
2.8 *Operation: modified prototype construction.*
2.9 *Operation: modified prototype evaluation.*
2.10 *Operation: preparation of final technical draft for manufacturing.*
3.1 *Operation: pre-series manufacturing.*
3.2 *Operation: elaboration of costs study.*
3.3 *Operation: design's adaptation to the producer's specific conditions.*
3.4 *Operation: quantity production.*
3.5 *Operation: product evaluation after a determined time of use.*
3.6 *Operation: introduction of eventual modifications based on the evaluation.*

This 24-steps skeleton can be generally used for the three types of project problems mentioned earlier (well-structured, moderately structured, ill-structured). However, the importance of the techniques that are to be applied changes.

The essential difference – as we have already seen – between a well-defined problem and an ill-defined problem, lies in the number of open and closed variables, both during the initial stage as in the final stage. Solving a not-quite-precise problem, the process of transforming open variables into closed ones, extends over more steps and does not end in step 1.5; this is similar to a procedure in the case of a moderately well-defined problem.

As can be observed, Bonsiepe does not differ by using the sequential arrangement, but through the refinement and precision of each stage. The author recommends not inferring from the sequential presentation that the design project has a horizontal and rigid sequence, but rather defines it as a iterative and recursive guide.

As a contribution to the designer's task, Bonsiepe describes some specific techniques, not as an exhaustive list, or a recipe, but as indicative recommendations:

- *Functional analysis*, to describe an object's functions, its components and interactions.
- *Morphological analysis*, as a combinatory technique for formulating possible sets of solutions for the same problem.
- *Synectics*, consists of tracking in order to locate other possible solutions to a problem, with actions such as analogy, inversion, amplification, miniaturization, substitution, empathy, etc.
- *Formal synthesis*, which indicated the perceptive aspects of an object: form, colour, texture, etc.
- *Optimizing use characteristics* through the location of criteria in relation to the user: ergonomics, safety, simplicity of use, cleaning, maintenance, access, etc.
- *Visualizing basic ideas* using visual codes: sketches, diagrams, graphs, models, prototypes; non-discursive and generally qualitative codes.
- *Modular coordination* through the measuring of object units or components with systematic numerations or series of geometric growth.

Last, Bonsiepe contributes a guide for the written formulation of a design project whose content may be:

– Introduction, which presents the argued motives that lead the project

- General goal, which points out the desired result
- Specific goal, which describes in detail the project's partial objectives.
- Work programme, subdividing into stages and actions
- Work plan where time is estimated according to stages
- Necessary human resources
- Approximate costs of staff, materials, construction of models, prototype, documentation, etc.
- Legal agreements on the manner of hiring, editing of finished work, etc.

Bonsiepe

1. Structuring of the problem

2. Design

Each stage subdivided into the following steps.

1.1 Operation: location of a necessity.

Technique (how to do it): to look for a situation of lookset in the population or the atmosphere for which the product to design will be destined.

1.2 Operation: valuation of the necessity.

Technique: to buy the necessity with others, with respect to its compatibility and priority.

1.3 Operation: analysis of the proyectual problem with respect to its justification

Technique: it can happen that a proyectual problem is false or is not justified. Comparing the function of the product to design with the proposal done by the sponsor, possible erroneous approaches are discovered.

1.4 Operation: definition of the proyectual problem in general terms

Technique: with base in compiled antecedents, describes to the function and the general objects of the project.

1.5 Operation: precision of the proyectual problem.

Technique: establish the specific requirements of the product and their subsystems settle down. The controlable and noncontrolable restrictions by the designer are formulated. The open variables become, as far as possible, in closed. The decision space draws up: specifications, material restrictions, processes of manufacture and costs.

1.6 Operation: subdivision of the problem in subproblems.

Technique: look for relatively independent problems to each other. To establish a division of functions.

1.7 Operation: hierarchial structuring of subproblems.

Technique: look for key functions or neuralgic functions. To establish a matrix of interaction between subsystems. To analyze its mutual dependency.

1.8 Operation: analysis of existing solutions.

Technique: to compare solutions according to its advantages and disadvantages. To establish a typology of existing solutions. To evaluate them according to a list of criteria, for example: complexity, costs, manufacture, security, precision, feasibility, technique, reliability.

2.1 Operation: development of alternatives or basic ideas.

Technique: "brainstorming", kinetic, morphologic analysis (box of Zwicky). Visualization of these ideas by means of drawings, schemes, scale models, models (that means, qualitative and nondiscursives codes).

2.2 Operation: examination of alternatives.

Technique: to put to the test each proposal of technical feasibility, functional, economic and formal, to collate advantages and disadvantages. For this aim provisional models are elaborated that simulate the details of the product at question.

2.3 Operation: selection of better alternatives.

Technique: assign values of qualification to a list of parameters, for example complexity, security, reliability, formal coherence, rank of costs, norms, simplicity of manufacture, duration. To choose or the alternatives with the highest score.

2.4 Operation: detail selected alternative.

Technique: measure pieces, determine processes of manufacture and materials, tolerances, completions. To prepare technical planes for the manufacture of the partial or total prototype.

2.5 Operation: construction of prototyping.

2.6 Operation: evaluation of the prototype.

2.7 Operation: introduce possible modifications.

Technique: with base in the test of the provisory product, to redesign or you sharpen the necessary details (that they were deficient).

2.8 Operation: construction modified prototype.

2.9 Operation: valuation of the modified prototype.

2.10 Operation: preparation of definitive technical planes for the manufacture.

3.1 Operation: manufacture of preliminary series.

3.2 Operation: elaboration of studies of costs.

3.3 Operation: adaptation of the design to the specific conditions of the producer.

3.4 Operation: production in series.

3.5 Operation: valuation of the product after a determined time of use.

3.6 Operation: introduction of temporary modifications with base in the valuation.

Textual/ Contextual Method

Jordi Llovet

Jordi Llovet's method is based on the theory of objects, which separates concepts that allow considering an object as the result of a design effort to reach the synthesis of the form. He considers what an object is and how it is created and concludes: that it is a formal synthesis that reunites its own space and, in it, a set of relations that constitute its particular complexity.

Jordi affirms that the methodology of design cannot limit itself to 'scientific' arrangement of the pertinences, because each object acquires and manifests its complexity in the environment. The analysis of objects must not avoid the situational context and its relationships with the synthetic form. He argues his methodological approach to design from semiology:

- Objects have a meaning, a plus of meaning that allows them to establish links among each other and form the so-called object system
- The object system can be framed by the communication outline
- A semiological analysis can be performed in that the object of design is considered equivalent to a text that can be spoken and written.

This methodological outline considers both the design text and context, without forgetting the peculiar relationships that each historical situation gathers; however, he does not provide a model because -affirms Llovet- the performance of objects is discursive in that it articulates in space paradigms that come form very different fields of pertinence.

Design works in a plural and polylogic manner, and so the act of designing involves formal, political, social, mercantile, psychological demands, among others, and the need to methodologically combine them as best as possible.[65]

Out of these considerations stands out the possibility of not reducing the designer's abilities into a specific method; it is proposed, if that were to be required, to unite methods that are already defined and synthesized.

It is considered that a design has two types of elements: *textual*, which are immanent and indispensable, necessary and sufficient for an object to become an entity, and *contextual*, which derive from the group of facts, data and situations that surround the object.

---

65 The application of Llovet's model requires a thorough study of the text *Design Methodology and Ideology*

In the textual field, a relatively operative semiologic approach is achieved by considering an object in the unification of several phrases.

Textualizing involves, based on a determined object typology, writing a text that is equivalent to the common aspects that define an object and those that specify it as a tool for another. Some examples of textual reduction:

The ***lamp***: *artefact that hangs from the wall, made of a spiral frame that hold a paper globe, provided with a lamp socket and a light bulb, whose main attribute is to provide light, with an electric line that goes from the lamp socket to the grid circuit that serves (the line) both as a support and a carrier of electricity, and is used (el artefact) to illuminate a dwelling.*

The ***toothbrush***: *instrument measuring 15 or 20 cm. long, composed of a flat bar (today) generally made of plastic, that has a large section to hold with the hand and a short section with some animal or plastic bristles that are very or little resistant to the touch, approximately one centimetre long, incrusted in the short section perpendicular to the flat side, forming two or three rows, with holes (optional) so that water would drain down the side corresponding to the bristles and another hole (also optional) in the opposite end of the bar so that it can be hanged from an exterior support; it can be of different colours, and serves, with prior (habitual) adding of a determined paste with certain characteristics, to wash teeth (generally one's own), more or less in all the visible surface according to an easily learned method that is not forgotten.*

In textualization, phrases that exhaustively define the features that characterize an object are articulated among each other by the language until achieving a text (syntactic and synthetic); the operation of reducing the object linguistically (describing its pertinences) has analytical implications that are necessary for the synthesis of form. The contextual or con-textual features are found within the text, although it is in the surroundings where they become contextualized and face the context characteristics.

Reducing something to text clears a set of factors that Jordi Llovet calls pertinent features, susceptible of being tabulated in the frame of pertinences as a moment previous to the synthesis of form.

The objective of the pertinences chart is to illustrate the obliged articulation of different discursive fields. This allows turning to one of the parts of the double operation that the realization of a design problem involves (graphic or object):

- Of analytical decomposition of the problem.
- Of articulation and synthesis of presuppositions, pertinent features or concrete variables.

Having seen the existing objects that offer a synthesis of pertinent features, the designer turns to a first series of characteristics in order to draw a logical scheme. In the first series, chaotic in principle (confusing mixture or *storming*), the characteristics are arranged according to the designer's criteria.

A sub-series of variables is established within a specific range of the general series. This sub-series, more or less exhaustive, is related to contextual aspects.

If the design problem were an oilcan, the first selected feature would be the material, the series of variables would be:

material: plastic, brass, aluminium, paper/cardboard/wood, stainless steel, crystal, ceramics

These variables would be related in this chart with the contextual demands, qualifying according to aptitudes with elemental signs:

+ good
± fine
→ 0 not good
0 absolutely no good

From the result of this chart, only possibilities that receive a qualification of acceptable suitability are kept. Thus a series of charts containing other features is developed: price, battery inclusion, aesthetic impact, etc.

a) material	plastic	brass	aluminun	paper, carboard wood	stainless steel	glass	cera mic
b) exigence of the content	+	+	+	→0	+	+	±
c) resistence to oxidation produced by oil &/or vinager	+	±	±	+	—	+	+
d) transparency, to distinguish the content	±	—	—	0	—	+	—
e) resistence of the material	±	+	+	→0	+	—	—
f) easy cleaning	—	+	+	→0	+	+	+

(+) good
(±) fine
(→0) not good
(0) absolutely no good

The previous contributes to the designer concluding a series of attributes, but does not guarantee all the aspects of the solution. To this regard, Jordi Llovet maintains that in design, there are no optimal or universal solutions. The text of an object of design can reach a high (optimum) qualification, however, the contextual factors (price, purpose, architectonic environment, consumer's taste) make the text realization impossible, the context involves the design problem in complex dialectics and so the optimization of the design frequently turns out an ideological fallacy.

Finally, the author advises in regards to his methodological contribution to the pertinence charts:

- Not to insistently hang on to existing synthetic solutions, to do that might cancel the possibility of an original funding, of reaching the invention.

- The pertinence chart is not delimited or closed, nor does it establish priority of value orders; the designer decides and controls, attending both to the object's set of pertinences (text) as to its context.
- The unpredictability of the pertinences in design hinders providing a model or 'scientific' arranging, variations must be considered in the processing of every specific problem.

Diana Model

Oscar Olea and Carlos González Lobo

The Diana Model and the General Model of the Process of Design constitute, in Mexico, the only serious attempts to introduce a methodological alternative that has pedagogically transcended in the different disciplines of design.

The Diana Model's principles lies in the definition of the demand that determines the designer's answer by integrating factors of location, destiny and economy (where, what for and with what), which contains information that is determinant of the most favourable form of the object-satisfier.

Form is the result of "comparing the factors of use with the factors of realization; the first, inherent to the object, the second, imposed by the designer's own ability and resources. These factors were defined as functionality, environmentality, expressivity, structurality and constructivity".[66]

These elements are followed by methodological arranging, as a sequence of recommendable arguments that involves a work, defined by the authors as dialectic in the dynamic relationship between reality and the subject who designs, from which the object results (dialectic agreement between necessity and possibility).

---

[66] The Diana Model is detailed in the work *Logical Analysis and Design* by architects Oscar Olea and Carlos González Lobo.

The process of design consists of the sequenced materialization of the verbal demand in an organized set of codifications and decodings whose coherence promotes a high degree of responsibility in the response, an element those points to the ethical principles of design.

For the configuration of the analytical model, Olea and González Lobo considered three entities involved in the problem of design:

- The *user*, with his single and not quite direct relationship with contemporary design.
- The *cultural entity*, mediating element that can be everything from a moral person to less concrete entities that act between the user and the object's realization.
- The *designer* himself.

Model description

Due to the complexity of Diana's Model, who comprehension demands practice, its description is based on the words of the authors of *Analysis and logical design*.

Demand: forms the user's needs by discerning the following elements:

- *Location*, which corresponds to the definition of the specific site where the need emerges: this is equivalent to determining its chronotopic coordinates (space-time).
- *Destiny* or finality that is pursued with the demand's fulfilment, includes design aspects as satisfying objects.
- *Economy* or evaluation of available resources: economical, technical, material and human.

D (demand) will be the integration of the U, D, E, vector that formalizes location, destiny and economy:

$$D = (U,D,E)$$

In order for the designer to find the adequate answer in the terms of demand (*problematic totality*) with his proposal (*realizable totality*), he must be capable of discerning the five levels of response that characterize the specific field of the design:

a) *Functional*, corresponding to the relationships between need and the form-function that fulfils it through use.
b) *Environmental* or relationship between the designed object and its environment and how it affects the object (altitude, temperature, etc.)
c) *Structural*, referring to the rigidity or durability of the object in relation to its use, relates the need's lifespan with the object's permanence in good conditions. Deals with the materials' resistance and the specific form in which they are adopted.
d) *Constructive*, contains problems when dealing with the production means and their incidence in the solutions
e) *Expressive*, concerning the strict aesthetic field; however, it is inescapably linked to functionality.

Following is a schematization of these concepts.

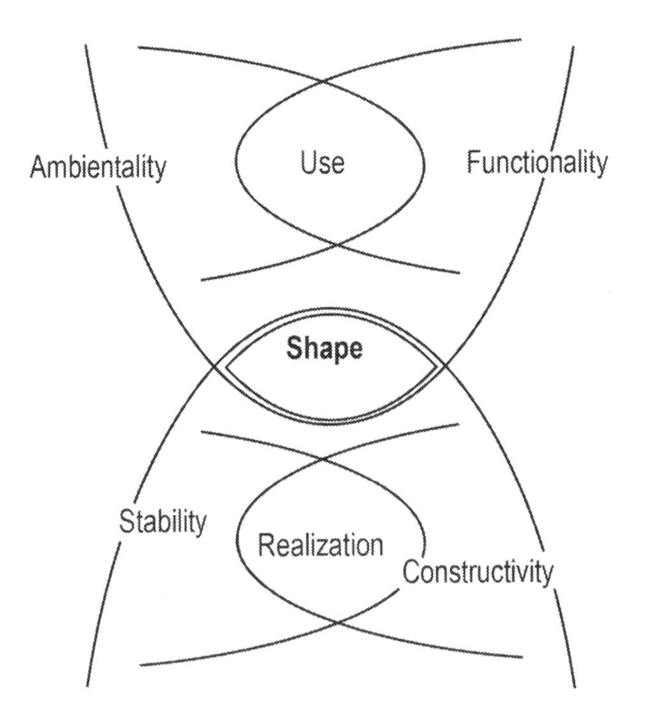

Analytical structure scheme:

Of the five levels described, *functionality and environmentality* correspond to *use, structurality and constructivity correspond to realization,* and expressivity is inherent to the *form.* The final form of an object of design results in an intersection between the set of use factors and the set of realization factors, as described in the following schemes:

If ***F*** is form and

fu	=	functionality,
am	=	environmentality,
est	=	structurality,
co	=	constructivity,
ex	=	expressivity,
U	=	use,
R	=	realization,

then:

U	=	*(fu, am)*
R	=	*(est,* co)

F= (U A R) ex; therefore, the process of design, that goes from a problematic totality to a realizable one, is made formal by the transformation:

D (U A R) V ex.

The signs *V and A* are the disjunctive "and/or" (see Latin) and the conjunctive "and" of the formal logic, respectively. (sic) [*it actually should sat conjunctive "and" and implicative "or" of the formal logic*]

This transformation operates through successive evaluations and decisions. The evaluations define the level of design and the decisions decide the level of propositions; both are integrated through the approach that orients solutions. This approach moves in search for design variables, within a logical universe of 15 regions (i, j) that are schematized by the matrix:

If we establish, finally, the following definitions:

U as "the demand situation",
D as "the demand purpose",
E as "the resources laid by the demand",

and, on a response level:

fu is the form that satisfies a use,
am is the form that is capable of regulating the function and its environment,
est is the permanent form in relation to use,
co is the realizable form, y
ex is the emotionally fulfilling form,

we could establish that in all the levels of response it is about finding a *form* that is adequate to each of these levels within a concrete demand, for which we must establish the links that allow joining the terms of demand with the following levels of response:

For the *location*, the link is *in*; for *destiny*, the link is *for*; and for *economy*, the link is *with*. And so:

fu v = Form that satisfies use in the demand situation,
am v = Form that regulates the function and its environment in the demand situation,
est v = Permanent form in the demand situation,
co v = Realizable form in the demand situation,
ex v = Emotionally fulfilling form in the demand situation,
fu D = Form that fulfils use for the purpose of demand,
fu D = Form capable of regulating the function and its environment for the purpose of demand,
est D =Permanent form for the purpose of demand,
co D = Realizable form for the purpose of demand,
ex D = Emotionally fulfilling form for the purpose of demand,

fu E = Form that fulfils a use with the resources imposed by the demand,
am E =Form capable of regulating the function and its environment with the resources imposed by the demand,
est E = Permanent form with the resources imposed by the demand,
co E = Realizable form with the resources imposed by the demand, and
ex E = Emotionally fulfilling form with the resources imposed by the demand.

The Diana Model is situated in the dominion of logic; its objective is to overcome criticism to the excessively theoretic and not very functional models. This demands of the designer a different rigor and his approach is directed toward the use of a computer as an auxiliary in the functions of data analysis and synthesis for which the computer is not indispensable.

The Diana Model, according to its authors, serves the designer for the following:

- Organizing the demand's structure.
- Defining his design approach or strategy.
- Establishing the propositional and decisive levels.
- Operating with rapidity in the search for possible solutions and their greatest efficiency.
- Regulating the entire logical process of design, allowing to tackle with relative facility highly complex problems of interdisciplinary nature.

For the use of the model, each step is directed toward the conclusion in specific forms that are shown after the description of the stages.

The stages are:

Demand configuration. – Looking up direct or complementary sources to gather information about the requirements.

Organization of the obtained information. – Integration of the data classification, distinction between information units in constants and variables.

Definition of the problem's analytical vector. – Selection of a certain number of variables according to a particular approach to the problem (for that, priority, secondary and accessory variables are distinguished).

Definition of the approach as a strategy. – Organization of variables so as to distinguish their interrelations, represented graphically to locate the dominion of each variable and delimit the dependent from the independent or interdependent.

Definition of the semantic areas of the terms of demand, which have a relationship with each variable. – Clarification of the formal fields of meaning that correspond to the different solution alternatives that each variable creates, in order to set aside the mute or irrelevant areas.

Organization of the research according to the defined semantic areas and, based on them, specification of the alternatives for each variable.

Assignation of probability of choice to each alternative of each variable represented by a set of fractions whose sum total is *one*.

Assignation of accumulative factor to each alternative.

Establishment of logical restrictions in the form of implicative arguments.

Binary qualification of the semantic areas of location, destiny and economy (defined in step 5) for each alternative based on objective criteria of acceptability.

Setting the lower limit of the probability of choice.

Data consignation in the codification sheet.

The Diana Model authors point out the following advantages:

- Turns the theoretic structure into an operative one.
- Does not require a high level of training in order to use.
- Coordinates the interdisciplinary work between the designer and his advisers.

- Forces a work method that amplifies by itself the vision that the designer might have of the problem.
- The computing process makes possible an exhaustive analysis of the alternatives in a short time.
- The designer is not required to have previous knowledge on computers or mathematics, beyond what his profession demands.
- The solutions specify an optimal degree and deficiencies in regards to the terms of demand.

The Diana Model is finally characterized as an instrument that facilitates the task of designing when dealing with complex problems with high-risk tasks and responsibility for the designer; however, its use is recommended in all cases in which objectivity, organization and control of the process of design are sought, actions that involve, without a doubt, methodological rigor.

General Model of the Design Process

UAM Azcapotzalco

The General Model of the Design Process is the result of a research conducted in the Division of Sciences and Arts for Design in Universidad Autónoma Metropolitana-Azcapotzalco, with the objective of defining a methodological alternative for the designer.

This perspective is based on two principles: the first refers to the analysis of the design situation along with the need for a national design and technology policy; the second refers to criticism of the current models of the design process.

The agreement on the need for national strengthening in the design task is interesting. The model attempts to be a step toward national self-determination in the field of design, as a scientific front in the face of the methodological alternatives of advanced and developed societies.

For the model specification, the grouping of disciplines in a single concept was considered as basis: grouped design or integrated design.

Design includes and integrates specialties such as architectonic design, industrial design, graphic communication design, urban design, etc.

Based on the idea of integration, the study of the process of design in each of the fields of design was initiated with the objective of pinpointing what is common between them.

This way, design was identified as "an integrated groups of professions that participate in a theoretical framework, a methodology and a technology that belongs to and is shared by all".[67]

According to a compilation presented by UAM-Azcapotzalco in the book *Against a dependent design*, the model's basic elements are the following:

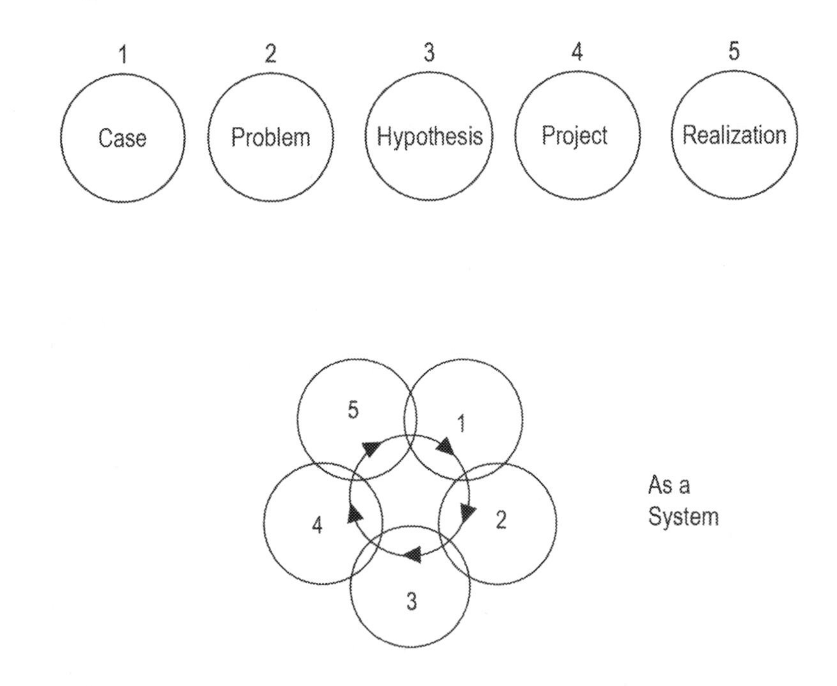

[67] The General Model of the Process of Design was developed as a methodological fundament of the studies of Design of the Graphic Communication in Universidad Autónoma Metropolitana Azcapotzalco with the collaboration of Felipe Pardinas –among other -, this work is compiled in the book *Against a Dependant Design*

Theoretical framework: understood as a group of propositions that constitute a body of knowledge of which action criteria result, which determine the totality of the sense of a system. It is integrated by three parts, as follows, namely:

Study field and objectives: referring to relationships between man and his environment through material objects that are useful in the life system.

Analysis instrument: which considers the multiple variables of the life system that affect each particular process of design and that make it so that the model accepts data entries and their interpretation. The process includes variables of both the life system and the context.

Practical application: according to the relationship of the theoretical framework with production materials and techniques.

Methodology: destined to point out operations, it results from the interrelation between the theoretical framework and data from the concrete reality, in order to integrate a systemized and rigorous whole that at the same time accommodates the designer's creativity; determines the relationships between the parts and the whole.

Technology: based on the consideration that the techniques must determine the real instrumental implementation (sic) of each of the parts.

In addition to the described elements, the design process requires cognitive contributions from other sciences in order to reach a concrete explanation of the design objects and their insertion into reality; there are two levels of interdisciplinary action:

Internal: which includes two types: *intra-design*, which considers the interactions of the different disciplines of design faced with the same problem and *extra-design*, concerning links between design and other disciplines that allow for the development and explanation of the designer's codes. Semiology and geometry are included in this level.

External: which responds to the access of design into theories, methods and techniques belonging to different disciplines such as sociology, psychology, medicine, engineering, etc., which contribute descriptive and constructive data to the solution of design problems.

The process developed by the General Model is composed of five stages whose flexibility makes them susceptible to evolution, thus, the sequence of the process of design must consider the determination of the problem and its solution and material realization alternatives; these steps are expressed in the following scheme, where:

- *Case,* treatment of the social phenomena through interdisciplinarity; from it, a design proposal is derived which includes a first integral formulation. The conditions established by the case will define the entire process.
- *Problem:* understands the phenomenon's study through the objects and, therefore, through the theoretic conditions of a discipline of design. Thus, the phenomenon is typified as a design problem with specific requirements for an action area.
- *Hypothesis:* includes the development of the maximum amount of alternatives for the problem's requirements. The purpose is to exhaust all possibilities and to choose the one that responds with the best aptitudes. The systems are analyzed so as to define alternatives: meaning in the *semiotic*, structure in the *functional*, definition of elements in the *constructive* and costs and implications in the *economic-administrative*.
- *Project:* formed by two parts: in the first, sketches, models and simulations are developed in an integral whole; in the second, they are compared with what was proposed in the hypothesis.
- *Realization:* corresponding to the material production of the proposed form.

One must keep in mind that each phase requires evaluation and feedback because the model is a cyclic sequence.

The model's flow programmatic diagram explains the sequence of sub-systematic operations of a design process, as follows: *MT:* Theorical framework. | *MET:* Metodology. | *T:* Techniques. | *SDR:* Data systems-requirements of a design demand. | *DR:* Data-requirements of a design demand. | *R:* Requirements. | *S:* System. | *EP:* Project elements of a design problem. | *REP:* Project requirements and elements of a design problem.| *SP:* Sub-systems of requirements and project elements. | O: Organization. | *Ts:* Technologies.

Other Models

Last, some models are included whose complexity makes it hard to provide a complete description and others have been proposed as schematic relations without foundation.

Christopher Alexander

Alexander compares three possible types of design:

- The first scheme represents the situation that is unselfconscious where the process only includes an interaction in two directions.
- The second scheme represents the situation that is self-conscious, where the design process is developed through interaction between the conceptual image and the context that the designer learns or invents, whose nature is unclear and based on intuition. In the process that is selfunconscious, it is not possible to mistakenly interpret the situation, simply because there is no representation of the context; in the process that is self-conscious, work is conducted based on a mental representation that is nearly always mistaken.
- The third scheme offers the possibility of setting aside partiality and retaining only abstract structural features: image arranged through defined operations that are not tied to the partiality of language and experience. Its development is achieved through mathematical entities: the sets (collections of things that may not have common properties and whose internal structure is assigned according to the problem that is being dealt with).

In the set theory, Alexander bases the representation of the problems of design in a way that the set is the particular analytical instrument that contains its varied elements.

Breaking down the sets into subsidiary sets or subsystems in a hierarchic sequence forms what the author calls a program, named this way

> [...] because it provides advice and instructions to the designer in regards to the subsets [...] which are his significant pieces, this way indicating which main aspects of the problem he must devote himself to. This program constitutes a reorganization of the manner in which the designer conceives the problem.[68]

The stages of the process according to this design program are:

- *Analytical* including the adequate design program for a particular problem. Its starting point is the requisite. The end product is a program or three of sets of requirements.
- *Synthetic* from which the form of the program is derived. This phase is also called the program's realization. Its starting point is the diagram and its end product is a diagram tree.
- *Solution* to the problem of design derived from an integrated description. The search for realization is given through constructive diagrams elaborated in the previous phase.

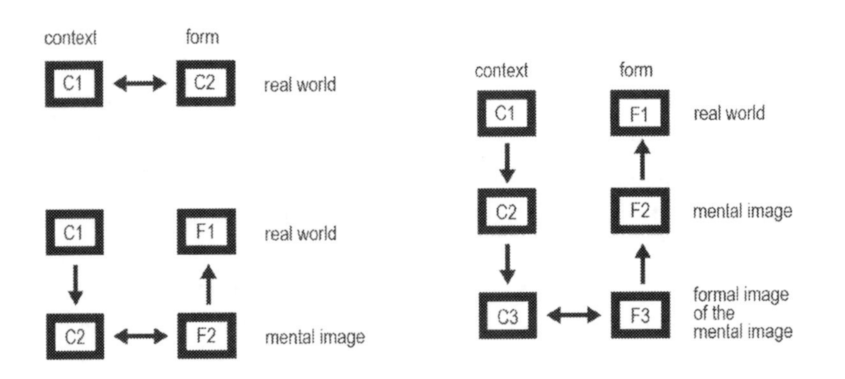

68 Read about this author in *Form Synthesis Essay*.

Morris Asimow

Scheme

Some design principles:

1. *Need:* the design must respond to individual or social needs that must be fulfilled.
2. Physically doable.
3. Economically affordable to do.
4. Can be financed in design, production and distribution operations.
5. The choice of a design concept must be the optimal one among the possible alternatives.
6. Optimization will be established based on design criteria.
7. *Morphology:* design as a progression from the abstract to the concrete.
8. *Process:* design is a iterative process of problem solving.
9. *Subproblems:* the problem solving depends of the subproblem solving.

Every design process must include the following elements:

- Information regarding a particular design.
- Theory of the design discipline.
- Evaluative function.
- Feedback.
- Course of action.
- Design or particular solution derived from the general principle.

The design process includes the following stages:

PRIMARY NEED

Design phase

Phase I Study of viability (intuitively determine a series of possible concepts)

Phase II Preliminary design (selection and development of the best concept)

Phase III Detailed design (concept description)
Phase IV Production planning

Production-consumption cycle phase

Phase V Distribution plan
Phase VI Consumption plan
Phase VII Retirement plan (during planning one evaluates and alters the concept according to production, distribution, consumption and product elimination requirements)[69]

The detailed design phase is subdivided into:

- *Design preparation*
- *Total design of subsystems*
- *Total design of components*
- *Detailed design of parts*
- *Preparation of ensemble drawings*
- *Experimental construction*
- *Product testing programs*
- *Analysis and prediction*
- *Redesign*

Finally, Asimow describes a general problem-solving process that he calls design process and which also has its stages:

1. *Analysis*
2. *Synthesis*
3. *Evaluation and decision*
4. *Optimization*
5. *Revision*
6. *Instrumentation*

---

[69] Morris Asimov, *Introduction to design*, p. 12

Archer's Scheme

A. Programming
B. Data collection
C. Analysis
D. Synthesis
E. Development
F. Communication[70]

Fallon's Scheme

1. Preparation
2. Information
3. Evaluation
4. Creativity
5. Selection
6. Project[71]

Gugelot's Scheme

1. Information stage
2. Research state
3. Design stage
4. Ruling stage
5. Assessment stage
6. Model realization stage[72]

---

[70] B. Munari. *Op. cit.*, p. 352

[71] Ibid.

[72] Jon Lang and Ch. Burnette. "Process Design Model" in M.L. Gutiérrez and others. *Against a Dependent Design*, pp. 221-229

Design process according to

Gillam Scott

1. First cause: human need.
2. Formal cause: imagine the how; provide the detailed mental image with a graphic expression.
3. Material cause: understand the nature of the materials and work with it, not against it.
4. Technical cause: manner in which the final form is given, with tools and machinery.[73]

Sidal's Scheme

1. Problem definition
2. Examination of possible designs
3. Limits
4. Technical analysis
5. Optimization/calculation/prototypes
6. Testing/final modifications[74]

---

73 Gillam Scott. *Design Fundamentals*, pp. 11-13

74 B. Munari, *Op. cit.*, p. 352

EMPHASIS IN GRAPHIC DESIGN. SEMIOTIC MODEL

Luz del Carmen Vilchis

Idea of the graphic design

Graphic communication finds the materialization of its expressive function in the designed. The designed is product of the task of representation. *Designing*, as a recreational behavior, *represents* reality; it is *mediation* in order to know reality from a certain point of view, and as any representation it is, due to its possibility, a representation for someone. The reference to this possibility is the peculiar aspect of the recreational nature of art, the hedonistic aspect that produces the representation that is manifested in the pleasure of knowledge, this way transformation acquires all its meaning, in the configuration, in the very act of establishing a language and opening it for interpretation.

Each piece of design, among other similar pieces, even when referring to the same theme and containing the same message, and using the same codes, is a variation of the representation; it is always possible to recognize in each designed object a free and arbitrary mediation, subject to what is called the critical scale of the correct representation, that is, the graphic repertoire that is pertinent to an adequate solution.

This is where the designer is considered an interpreter and not a mere imitator of a model, and this is also where the relationships between the designed and the creator of the designed can be understood.

This does not mean that the mimesis is cancelled; it takes place as it contains the cognitive sense of the essence, thus exhibiting the nature of representation. Imitation is such if it repeats, that is, if it copies. Imitation is mimesis when it re-presents, that is, when it cognizes and re-cognizes. Representation as a recreational process involves the receivers of the designed; it is the moment in which the graphic communication is understood, when the whole of meaning can be manifested.

The designed, as a representation, does not belong to the represented, it belongs to the way in which it is (re)presented, it has a referential structure that gives access to the representation of "something", as a visual image it represents, in the form of reproduction, an appearance mediated by a concept.

One should be careful of the possible reduction from the concept of understanding to mere sympathy or empathy because understanding is not necessarily an act of congeniality; the receiver keeps a distance from the designed, which prevents him from having a pragmatic participation. This refers to the very act of seeing, where the aesthetic game includes the spectator and involves time and distance in which it can be excluded.

The previous is applicable to the aesthetic dimension of the designed; however, we must consider the communicative being behind which there are a great number of receivers who, although they represent the same number of possibilities of the message, there must be coincidence in the understanding of this message, otherwise the designed will not fulfil its function.

It must be stated that one of the designer's intentions when translating a message into graphic images is to achieve the receiver's congeniality in the marrow of the visual text, or at least with the context of the designed. An agreement must be reached in the conversation between the receiver and the designed, of which there are two types:

previous, in that there must be a common tradition, an agreement on the language's participation, and factual, where congeniality becomes obvious, patent.

Thus two interpretation poles are established, that of the message itself carried out by the designer, and the concretion conducted by the receiver. Design cannot be exclusively identified with any of the two exegeses as it is more than the visual text itself and only acquires meaning in its concretion, it cannot become independent of the receivers' contributions, which, at the same time, are conditioned by the dispositions of the visual text.

The designed defines its essence through the surplus of meaning, which allows it to transcend and to be interpreted once and again and re-presented in permanent chains of graphic communication. The design is manifested in a metaphorical task in which it cannot be affirmed that all that is stated by the message is stated by the issuer, even if the message has an elaborate and deliberate approximation. The design object contains the message and reaches the receivers who interpret it; the graphic message undergoes changes that, in spite of the limits of their determination, have a multitude of interpretations by the receiver.

Graphic design is based on the development of a visual text, in which understanding is reached through interpretation. When it is perceived, this perception is enlightened, in it lies the interpretation, this interpretation being important in contexts that are different from those of the receiver and the moment of interpretation. In fact, as an expression, design exhibits a *locutionary* or *syntactic level* (how the visual text says it), an *illocutionary* or *semantic level* (what the visual text says) and a *perlocutionary* or *pragmatic level* (for what and for whom it is said), useful categories to situate the possible links of the interlocutor. Translating the expression of the designed is the dialogic possibility, connection between the outside and the inside, and vice versa.

The basis for the dialogic relationship is the question-answer figure, the question being the most important. Asking a question opens up and makes possible the manifestation that could be the object.

Therefore, the understanding of a graphic communication must be understood as part of a meaning taking place, in which meaning is formed and concluded; in this process, temporality plays a transcendent role, thus, understanding refers to a process that is always open, never ending nor structured.

The process of understanding is an intellectual act that alludes to the epistemological alternatives that adhere to conceptual circumstances that allow distinguishing what is convenient from what is inconvenient, alluding to the individual's ethical tasks. The opening up to the possibilities of understanding design objects must start with knowledge of their intra and interdisciplinary relationships, whose whole integrates the conceptual structure that corresponds to the discipline's theoretical dimension.

The development of visual communication has given way to conceptual transpolation from other disciplines and to the generation of its own conceptual structure that allows basing and explaining its different manifestations, understanding graphic design as a creative discipline that emanates from a type of socioeconomic system; it is not a simple circumstantial profession, it is, to quote André Ricard, the result of updated and specialized persistence and of the human being's congenital ability to obtain the elements that are necessary for his cultural survival.[75]

In recent decades, the transcendence of communication and significance theories in the field of design stands out, because in addition to explaining the need to fulfil demands of rationality in design – according to which it is possible to think of signs integrating a way of transforming things, in order to create realities that lead to other realities–, this field of knowledge has made possible the extrapolation of some linguistic and semiotic theories to the theory of the image, thus the terms of its understanding have expanded.

---

75 André Ricard, *Design Why?*, p. 183

Semiosis and Sense

Semiosis[76]: is the possibility of using the sign, that is, it refers to a fundamental characteristic of human behavior, the ability to evoke, represent or refer to something, all the relationships between the word and the meaning (or form of the expression and form of the content) that are included in the sign.

Understood as the process in which formal elements operate as signs and therefore are susceptible to interpretation, this concept allows us to explain the configuration of any visual message as well as its social behavior as an object of meaning through the three possible dimensions indicated by Charles Morris:

- *Syntax*: determined by the possible formal relationship between some signs and others, it includes the rules of organization and composition that determine the permissible combinatorial ranges of the fundamental visual elements; it reaches its most specific and concrete manifestation in the diversity of styles that have impacted the visual communication. As a last resort, it is the systematized relationship among visual signs. In semiotic definitions, this aspect is acknowledged through syntactic rules.
- *Semantics*: involves the possible relationships between visual signs and the objects or ideas to which they are applicable, it surpasses the original idea that it solely corresponds to conceptual images or to intermediation with benchmarks – things–, by virtue of the complexity of visual communication, which gives rise to a polysemic condition in which the surpluses of meaning constitute the messages' main characteristic.
- *Pragmatics*: involves the possible relationships between signs and interpreters in which there are two angles: the first describes links between the need, the message and the designers, and the second is exclusively interested in links between the perceivers, receivers or users of the design and the visual communication objects.

[76] Charles Morris. *Signs Theory Fundamentals*, pp. 27-41

It is impossible to understand the development terms of visual language if its group of signs lacks syntactic dimension, and so a sign is characterized by its relationships with the remaining signs, with the objects, and with the users in the so-called formation rules, which determine the independent and permissible relationships of the elements of a visual set, and the transformation rules that determine the visual sets that can be obtained from the basic visual sets.

The previous is feasible in the elemental classification of signs into levels of semantization: indexical signs, which can mean a single idea or object (a square); characterizing signs, these can have plural meanings and therefore be combined in different ways that explain or limit the reach of their application (a man); and universal signs, which can mean anything whose relationships are open to any sign and have universal implication (an arrow).

Sense: is the concept that includes all the acceptations or meanings that integrate in the interrelations of codes a visual text in the framework of a particular discourse; this is possible due to the multivocal condition of the designed. Design takes on different meanings according to the political, economical, personal or social conditions and circumstances of its interpretation. The designed is multivocal –it always presents more than one meaning–, design is polysemic –it always presents more than one sense–.[77]

A main meaning –associated with the message's nucleus–, secondary meanings –associated with the message's syntactic and expressive conditions–, contextual meanings –dependent on the conditions and contacts in which the communication is immersed–, sociocultural meanings –related to habits, costumes, knowledge, and experiences–, and affective meanings –linked to emotional aspects–, are identified in a graphic communication.

Ambiguity: in a graphic design object can cause the *unconscious transference of meaning* –indiscriminate mobility of meanings–, or an alteration in the possible ranking of the different meanings.

---

[77] Luz del Carmen Vilchis, *Design: Knowledge Universe*, p. 40

The staging of design does not authorize an interpretation of its meaning in any form, the receiver's relationship with the designed is not cathartic –elimination of memories and references–, but it is an *anagnorisis* –the action of re- cognizing–, that is, although design has a surplus of meaning, it will always be conditioned to the formal an stylistic conjugation of its elements –it is not possible to interpret what is not fixed in the object–, even if it is considered a residue and is contextualized in another time and place, interpretation will not be limited.

Text and context

Graphic design is understood here as a text,[78] that is, a pertinent communication unit, by which an isolated sign or a group of signs are not understood (the letter and the word, in linguistic theory), but a structured and coherent block of signs that incorporates the communicative intentions of a visual design whose articulatory elements are indiscernible because it constitutes a communication strategy and has specific pragmatic intentions; to disarticulate it would result in the message's tergiversation.

Image, under the determinants of communication strategies, becomes visual text; it is the graphic message fixed in a printed support that produces the visual expression. However, we must acknowledge in the text an existence that is linked to the context and hence to the multiple discursive answers that it could manifest from its relationship with what is real. Thus, the concept of text is linked to the idea of discourse, understood as a maximum unit of determinants of the visual text, which is the reason why it is possible to understand the text through analysis units –grammar of the visual text–, or through the set of procedures that determine a discursive continuum – the semantic-syntactic representation–.

And so, we speak of the understanding of text based on the image's syntactic and perceptive properties beginning with the concepts of unity and coherence; in these terms, it is possible to elaborate a textual analysis

78 *Cfr.* Roland Barthes. "From piece to text" in Barthes, *Le Bruissement de la langue*, pp. 69-78.

based on the *theories of visual literacy* (analysis of the image through the syntactic relationships of the signs that integrate it),[79] *iconism* (analysis of the image in its relationship with reality) and *isotopies* (analysis of the image based on equivalent images in a determined space).

The context: refers to all the reality that surrounds a sign, an act of visual perception or discourse, either as knowledge of the issuers, as experience of the receivers, as physical space, as a group of objects, as environmental conditions or as an activity. The context is made of all the visual or non-visual mediations of expression, likewise as a whole, it is made of the complete situation that surrounds an image and determines a meaning. The reference and analysis of the total context must show what is implicit in it, interpret it, and then integrate it to the explicit –the designed–, thus achieving meaning.

A whole context in the graphic communication work relates the main features of the participants –persons, personalities–, the participants visual action, the participants non-visual action, the relevant objects, the non- visual and non-personal events, and the effect of the visual action. This complex can be understood integrated by visual context, discursive context, situational context, regional context, emotional context and cultural context.

Semantic field, lexical field and functions

First, we must distinguish the lexical field from the semantic field,[80] the first refers to all the words that designate the same sector of reality (for example, the lexical field of serigraphy or the lexical field of computers), whereas the second, which is more complex, involves the categories, concepts and verbal or visual signs that mark the perimeter and the sense of a fragment of reality or of knowledge.

In order to understand the different phenomena of graphic communication, one must start with the definition of the *semantic field* of

---

[79] D. A. Dondis. *Image Syntax*, pp. 9-12

[80] Alejandro Del Palacio. *Neoliberalism and revolution. Crisis and need for change*, pp. 25-27

each one of these phenomena since they correspond to different fields of knowledge and hence to different languages; if we understand that each language builds its own semantic field and, with it, the specific limits and way of naming, explaining, and understanding the aspect of the world that one wishes to explain, it would be clear that the conditions for the possibility of knowing each of the phenomena of graphic communication involve specific categories that allow mediating between the semantic field of this discipline and the semantic field of the interdisciplinary relationship to which it alludes, until establishing a common semantic field with which the pertinence of any affirmation or argumentation can be decided. It is impossible to have a clear understanding of the phenomena if one does not understand the consequences of the semantic fields.

Each conscious configuration within the framework of communicative action performs a series of functions or variables dependent on the designer, the text and the context; conceptually, these originate in the theory of functions of R. Jakobson but have found an application extendable to non- verbal communication forms.

The following functions can be considered: referential or intellective and objective formulation of a message in relation to a referent; emotional or transmission of the emotional and subjective attitudes of the internal issuer in regards to the referent: taste, interest or abstraction; conative: semantic and pragmatic, determines the possible interpretations that the receiver makes of the message, that is, refers us to the surplus of meaning in the communication; expressive or poetic, which lies in the plastic, hence, aesthetic qualities of a visual discourse; metalinguistic, which specifies the codes that are used to refer to –already existent–, object-languages, this is the case of the verbal language translated into the typographic code and the photographic language translated into the photographic code, and phatic, which emphasizes the message through resources of redundancy, reiteration, remarking, repetition of some element so as to catch the receiver's attention, thus it refers to the surplus of meaning that exceeds the limits of the message itself –including its semantization–, to guarantee perception.[81]

[81] Jord Llovet. *Op. cit.* pgs. 97-98

Visual grammar: Discourses / Genres / Codes

Discourse: is the maximum unit of determinants of the visual text; it is conditioned in the visual communication by the aims to which it is destined. Each deliberate form of proceeding involves a specific and characteristic way of building and organizing the messages. Each of the visual discourses is understood as a communication system that requires its peculiar forms of showing issuers, messages and receivers, in which the forms of response can only find their efficiency in themselves. Thus, factors of relevance are those which define discourses where resources, such as rhetoric,[82] also acquire a meaning within the framework of similitude and coexistence with other languages, such as the verbal, to which one appeals as consistent support for the messages.

In graphic communication, the following discourse typology can be established:[83]

- *Advertising discourse,* integrates the relationships between the designed image and the commercial thought, it is manifested in all forms of expression of advertising and its objectives are linked to promoting objects, products and services that are understood as merchandise or promoting people whose activities are considered a commodity (show business).
- *Propagandistic discourse,* integrates the relationships between the designed image and the political thought, it is also known as political imagery and its goals focus on the persuasion or promotion of ideas, its form of response is manifested through vote or manifestation.
- *Educational discourse,* integrates the possible relationships between the designed image and the purposes of the didactic communication that are focused toward formal –school related–, or non-formal –non-school related–, education, which involves all the aspects of learning: family, street, printed

---

[82] Daniel Prieto. *Design and Communiccation.* p.145

[83] Luz del Carmen Vilchis, *Op. cit.* pp. 46-53

means, audiovisual aids, etc.-, the perceivers' response is in the tangible modification of behaviors.

- *Plastic discourse:* integrates the relationships between the designed image and the aesthetic and recreational thought, it is inserted into visual arts as part of the so-called graphics.
- *Ornamental discourse:* integrates the relationships between the designed image and ornament functions, it is related to decorative arts and arts and crafts.
- *Perverse discourse:* manifested in all graphic communication genres that intentionally cause damage –visual (perceptual), moral or intellectual–, to the receivers, corrupting their habitual purposes.
- *Hybrid discourse:* those that result from the joining of two different discourses, they are considered confusing in that there is an overlap of intentions that is translated into the possible fragmentation of both the message and its results; the best example of this are recent political campaigns that have used rhetorical resources in their advertising campaigns, resulting in a coarse and improbable communication.

Within the discourses the different levels of veridiction are manifested, these are associations of the image with the connotation of truth, based on which the following are defined: true discourse, which corresponds directly to the facts, truthful; veracious discourse, which partially adjusts to the true discourse, that is, it includes some truth; probable discourse, adjusting to the rules of a genre and appearing true, it does not offer any kind of falseness; improbable discourse, does not appear true and can offer some kind of falseness.

The idea of genre allows us to conceive the different discursive manifestations of the design of the graphic communication in the taxonomy of means that are organized by their physical characteristics and their conditions of configuration, production and reproduction.

This point of view allows a differentiation between the diversity of objects that comprise the designed in graphic communication, grouping them in the following genres: editorial (printed objects whose graphic design depends on continuous text); *paraeditorial* (printed objects whose graphic design originates from a minimum text, generally reduced to brief and specific information); *extraeditorial* (printed objects whose graphic design originates from a specific subject, they may or may not integrate text, however, this text is always conditioned by the image); *informative and indicative* (printed objects whose graphic design is based on image, providing information even though they lack text; they tend to use symbolic representation and their permanence is long-term); *ornamental* (printed objects whose graphic design is based on simple morphological elements, these objects do not provide information and lack text, they tend to use repetitive patterns; *linear narrative* (printed graphic manifestations whose interpretation basis is manifested through drawing; when including text, it is conditioned by the narration itself); and *non-linear narrative* (graphic manifestations whose interpretation basis is manifested through drawing and text, organized based on digital language, their reading is electronic, limited by conditions laid by surfing and interactivity).

Within the *codes*, groups of relevant elements are defined and classified based on which the graphic communication system is formed, through combination according to basic preset rules; the relevant elements of the codes are called signs and their own conditions make possible the articulation of messages.

The articulation of the different graphic communication codes creates a structure in which the codes are constituent elements, where the modification of one involves the modification of another and the consequent alteration of the sense in the communication. Graphic communication has the following codes: *morphologic* (including both formal abstract schemes as well as formal configurative elements); *chromatic* (including the coloured schemes that are given to a certain design); *typographic* (including all the characterized texts) and *photographic* (including original or manipulated photographic images).

Visual grammar and articulation

Visual grammar[84] is one of the moments in the understanding of the graphic design, its articulation designates any activity or form of

[84] Teun A. Van Dijk. *Discourse Structure and Functions,* pp. 77-81

semiotic organization that a designer performs in order to form new units of meaning; it is firstly understood as the display of the form's syntactic possibilities, obligatorily implicating its semantic and pragmatic interrelations. It determines or proposes relationship procedures of the graphic communication codes, integrating:

Articulation fundamentals, which in turn comprise the principles of diagramming, which start with the design's spatial determination, the format's geometric fragmentation conditions, this is the main support where the organization of the formal elements and the *principles of classification* lie, it starts with the spatial ranking of the design dependent on the format conditions. In this support, the components of the *formal articulation* and of the *conceptual articulation* are developed.

Formal *articulation develops* the relationships between: *visual alphabet*: including all the morphological elements or components of a configuration: form (point, line, outline, plan, volume), texture, color (shade, saturation, brightness); *dimensional elements*: referring to characteristics of size, scale and proportion, and the determinations for proposing first, second and third dimensions, and structural elements: referring to the possible relationships of the morphological and dimensional elements: perspective, direction, symmetry, regularity, juxtaposition, interposition, sequence and grouping.

Likewise, the *formal articulation* integrates values such as *degree of iconicity* and *figurative degree*. The first is the degree of realism of an image as compared to the object that it represents, and the second refers to the names designated to the representation values of the form of the objects or beings of the world that are recognized through visual perception.

Conceptual Articulation explains the links between the *composition laws* (rules that condition the relationships that exist between the structural elements, which are created from their qualities and conditions, they prescribe what must be done or what must be omitted in a configuration: law of proximity, law of similarity and equality, law of closure, law of continuity or common destiny, law of experience, law of meaning, law of figure-background, laws of perspective, laws of gravity, laws of contrast, chromatic laws), *structure values* (qualities that must satisfy the formal structures: harmony, rhythm, equilibrium, movement, depth, tension, contrast, unity, synthesis, order and their possible variations or alterations, this is called *anamorphosis* and includes distortion, de-structuring, fragmentation, etc.) and *semantic characteristics* (meanings that result from a configuration: subtlety, integrity, audacity, activity, passivity, abstraction, transition, etc. and their possible opposites).

These components of graphic design –message, composition, support, configuration and communicative conditions–, undergo transformations according to the different networks that are formed from the contexts, space, time, and form, and each one of them affects the cultural environment.

Graphic design, as a part of visual communication, responds to diverse purposes; each discourse is directed toward a certain type of receiver, defined through internal issuers, contents and rhetorical resources whose processes integrate the relationships of the designed image with the diversity of sociocultural thoughts and behaviors. For the previous, this framework of knowledge allows understanding and explaining the design objects based on an interdisciplinary conceptual structure. This is a conceptual proposal that presents the systematization of the elements that comprise the visual language in graphic design. For this purpose, knowledge in linguistics, communication, semiotics, and hermeneutics are applied in a knowledge network that results in a visual grammar, a theoretic approach to the real structures in communicative interactions.[85]

---

[85] *Cfr.* Luz del Carmen Vilchis, *Op. cit.*

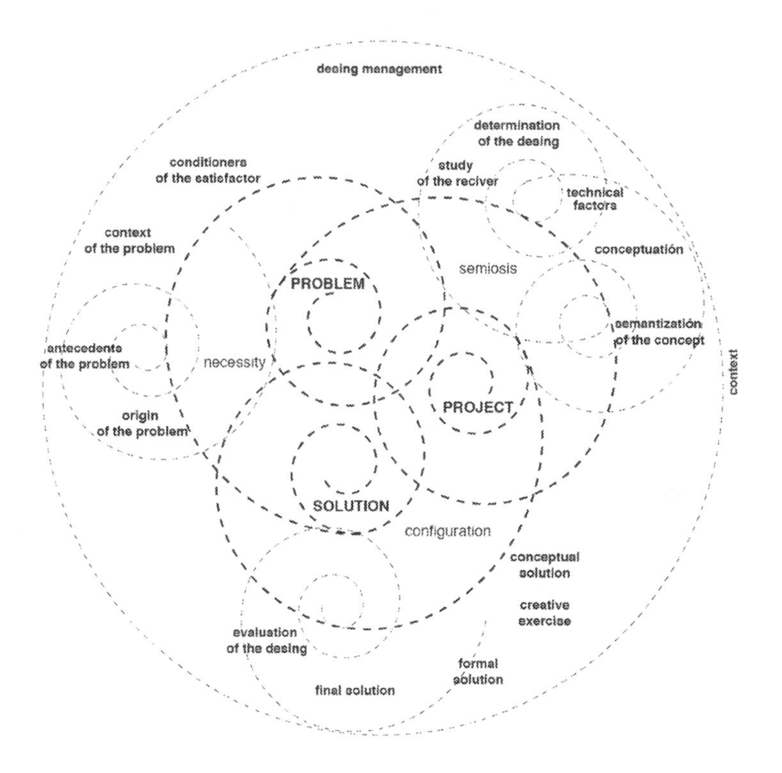

To understand a problem of graphic communication, it must be said from a natural or legal entity in which a specific necessity arises. We need to define or describe:

• Source of the problem: specific need for communication

- *Current status of communication*: describe the communication conditions in which it is embedded the necessity
- *Definition of the need to*: clarify what is and what its characteristics, its causes and consequences and expectations that provide a solution
- *Circumstances*: situations immediately preceding the necessity, or associated with it

• Problem Background:

- *Previous state*: how the necessity was generated, how and why was chosen to determine it as a problem

- *Previous solutions*: to characterize foregoing alternatives from the current necessity expression
- *Sequentiality*: it belongs to a series, features of this and previous message line

• Problem Context

- *Factors that affect the necessity*: specify those social elements, materials or technical from the problem context (which are related with)
- *Resources*: detailing the scope and any kind of material, human or technical resources in place to achieve the purposes of external transmitter
- *Spatiotemporal constraints*: requirements and possibilities of message permanence

• Satisfier Conditioners

- *Message*: define what transmitter want to communicate, first the idea or concept and second overall amount of information to include in the message. It means to approximate the idea of verbal records in terms of quantity, quality, availability and reliability
- *Intentionality*: describe the external transmitter purposes in short, medium and long time limit –to sell, promote, persuade, raise awareness, inform, teach, etc.- in terms of synchrony and diachrony
- *External Transmitter*: specify the sponsor or responsible for communicating the message and define its guidelines, intentions and constraints to the project
- *Internal Transmitter*: specify who, directly or indirectly will communicate the message in the media. Could be: person(s), character(s), company, brand(s), institution, sign(s) or receiver(s)
- *Receptor*: describe the specific audience you are addressing the message, predefine residence requirements, proximity possibilities and frequency indicators

The correct interpretation of a design problem is then detailed knowledge of the nature of necessity, is not yet to have a look at the problem, project competition, but may state the same corpus. The designer should not assume that any relationship of necessity is a logical starting point. Understanding the problem always include, never exclude or assume, or make value judgments *a priori;* designers analyze the facts surrounding the communication phenomenon. Nor have attitudes involve subjective as taste or regulatory references limiting knowledge as this leads to previous interpretations.

Described and located the necessity and communication intention, one must accept that the project is a complex process for which the correct interpretation of the problem should be based on a conscious effort to make intelligible the internal conditions that determine the necessity and the external variables that condition.

Methodological Development of the Project

Defined the design problem, the next step in the *methodological structure,* known as the *design process,* is the project integration and specify the frame or set of fundamental relations that correspond to currently defined moments based on a logical sequence.

All these considerations make clear that the complexity of the design methodology assume that the analysis of the problems is undoubtedly important, because without it, the design process would be inconsistent, arbitrary and meaningless, the process is still based on a method by itself, it doesn't reach the final configuration of the object, it defines and limits, but does not solve creatively.

The form is contained in the determinants but must be deciphered and structured in the appropriate media, the real design work is the transformation process that has until now any methodology arcane, no model has yet proposed techniques to make this process conversion.

The lack of methodological support and the use of unfounded ambiguous models without theory conduct the designer to make absurd proposals of solution that not only don't provide any benefit to society but, instead, generate irrational problems and divert of technical and human resources in meaningless companies.

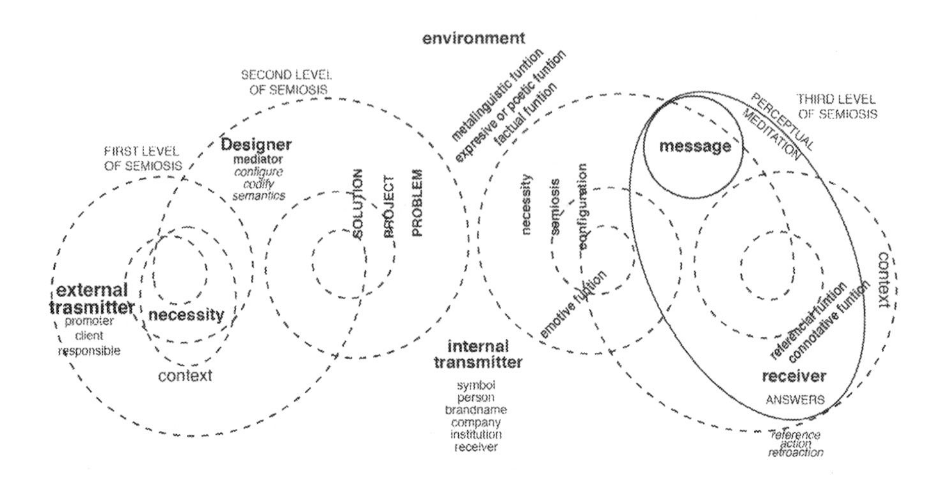

The best proof of this lies in the enormous number of problems whose solution claims to have been founded on projects. Also generate unsolved problems creating visual pollution conflicts, values deterioration and perceptual degradation of the receptor.

The project must submit their possible actions:

• *Design Management:* this is a constant in design process, manifested with different intensities; it involves actions to project management:

- *Relationship with the Customer*: highlights actions about problem knowledge, awareness the needs of communication, understanding and consensus on the draft
- *Work Plan*: summarizes, define and schedule actions to develop the outcome potential (never ensure, nor has the formal characteristics from the outputs)
- *Material Assessment Process*: define the material scope and develop the budget
- *Obtaining Resources*: define terms of contracts and collection of design

• *Receptor Study:* integrate all the personal and social characteristics of the receiver as well as those relevant conditions to the phenomena of perception, communication and meaning

- *Physical Factors*: age, rhythm and form of reading, reading level, reading speed, physical limitations, environmental conditions of reading, rhythm of activity, mobility opportunities, possible factors of proximity to various types of communication (manual, door or wall, street, etc.), physical characteristics such as height and field of view
- *Psychological Factors*: identification of behavior, levels of understanding of knowledge, psychological constraints, holding capacity, repeatability, characteristics and concentration limits and continuity
- *Cultural Factors*: education, vocabulary limits, limits of legibility, local behavioral characteristics, social critics, habits (individual), customs (social) credibility variables (age, sex, stratum, level of education, political affiliation, powers physically and mentally affected, etc..), critical social and ideological aspects

• *Determination of the Graphic Communication:* indicate the conditions of the message from the conceptual structure of graphic communication

- *Definition of Graphic Discourse*: decide which of the speeches corresponds with the message intention specifying the possible rhetorical issues
- *Gender Definition*: decision about the appropriate gender to satisfy the necessity, accounting belongings as dependent and independent variables of the design problem in terms of function: ability to understand, context integration, accessibility, reliability.
- *Style Definition*: decision about style, must consider intentional, receiver characteristics, and gender discourse.

• *Technical Factors:* operational issues that could affect the process such as

- *Printing Systems or Integration*: define, depending on destination-traditional or digital-to be set in the middle, the determinants, limitations and implications of a selected system
- *Operating Conditions*: check technical and technological contingencies that affect the process

- *Material Conditions*: involves making decisions about special media, if necessary, requires technical evidence

• *Conceptualization:* main concepts of project

- *Message*: idea (what means), must integrate all constituent features of objects, ideas or concepts
- *Verbal Message Expression*: *text base* (idea), *anchor text* (ideas that link the concept of the message), *secondary texts*, *informational texts* and *legal texts*.

• *Preview of the concept*

- *Main Image*: image is identified with the core or essence of the message
- *Secondary Images*: images that would enlist any connection with viewing the message or text

• *Concept Semantization:* process by which problem determinations and message contents are incorporated in the form of meanings. These are the terms of the graphic communication means, the semantics is the result of selection and combination of conceptual options

- *Veridiction Level*: possible association of the image to the connotation of truth in its various possibilities: true discourse, true, plausible and implausible
- *Meaning Definition*: specification of the possible message connotations

  ➢ *Main direction*, that of greater determinateness
  ➢ *Secondary Sense* concomitant ideas that can evoke an image of a regular or instinctive
  ➢ *Sense emotional or affective content*, reactive feelings or sensations caused by images

- *Semantic Universe*: possible actors, functions, qualities and aspects of semantic fact, reality has a perimeter of which are located in the act or acts that contain the message

- *Timing*: possible location of semantic fact or a chronological event data

• *Ethical Review*: valuation of the consequences and axiological implications of the semantic concepts, this act refers to the comparison between concepts, means, ends and conclusions regarding their mutual adaptation to the potential benefits or harm to the receiver.

CONCLUSIONS

The human condition is essentially characterized by the use of reason – an innate quality that allows individuals to exercise common sense and good judgement, and to have the ability to infer and deduce. However, sadly, sociocultural determinants cancel, inhibit and occasionally distort such qualities. The training of knowledge in the spheres of logic and, hence, in the field of methodology, is the most important resource to steer judgement and reflection and the actions that derive from them, in benefit of the development of comprehension.

Methodology is the sustenance of all disciplines. Comprehending that it is based on the indissoluble epistemological, logical and operative links between theory, method and technique, and that its foundations derive from general methodology, allows us to understand the transcendence of thought structures and to avoid the equivocations that give rise to empty, unfounded methods in different fields of knowledge.

It is not possible to determine that a given method is more valid than another - thus involving reductionism, because any of these methods *per se* is just a model that acquires meaning and sense at the precise moment in which it is ascribed with congruent contents, with a thought process of which approach may be directed toward research, technical realization, or creation. What is important is that the theory that is related to this model be coherent with the thought of the individual who applies it.

Methodological models have been proposed for the benefit of human beings, it is not human beings who should adapt to a certain model - this action has no reasoning whatsoever and implies an indicative and imposing stance.

One cannot direct the generation of knowledge based on form; the implicit background is what comprises the different aspects of a discipline and directs them in the specificities of the method.

In design, a methodological model is the gnosiological route of which purpose is to perform actions pertaining to research, either to solve a problem regarding an object of study or to solve a necessity. In other words, it is a series of indicators that guide both thought and action. Design methods are the part of methodology that is organized and systematized by elements based on which a project's trajectory is decided. The principles and constants on which a method is based will allow the designer to choose a specific constant that will determine the theoretical and practical results of the research.

Conceptual structures and pragmatic procedures are the inherent and primordial extremes of design methodology, and methods are models whose arrangement and framework have been proposed based on cardinal theories and significant factors that guide them toward any of the factors that determine a designer's thought, such as: problem, necessity, user, creativity, form or function.

Likewise, intra and interdisciplinary theories lead the designer's criterion in particular circumstances that are defined based on the model and shaped with their contents. The characterization of thought and action in design is expressed in these methodological sequences and in their results. Only based on the previous do disciplines transform and grow, modifying their contribution to the different fields of culture.

BIBLIOGRAPHY

- *Ackoff*, Rusell L. *Redesigning the Future*. Mexico, Ed. Limusa, 1981.
- *Alexander*, Christopher. *Form Synthesis Essay*. 4a. ed. Buenos Aires, Eds. Infinito, 1976
- *Alonso*, José Antonio. *Methodology*. Mexico, Edicol, 1977
- *Ander-Egg,* Ezequiel. "Introduction to research techniques" in *Social Sciences Methodology*. Mexico ENEP-Acatlán, 1979
- *Aróstegui,* J.M. and others. *Methodology of scientific knowledge*. Mexico, Latin American Presence, 1981.
- *Asimow,* Morris. *Introduction to Design*. USA, Prentice-Hall Inc., 1962.
- *Barthes*, Roland. "From piece to text" in Barthes, *Le Bruissement de la langue*. Paris, Seuil, 1984.
- *Baudrillard*, Jean. *Critique of Political Economy of the Sign*. 2a. Mexico, Siglo XXI Eds., 1977
- *Baudrillard*, Jean. *Objects System*. 3a. ed., Mexico, Siglo XXI Eds., 1977
- *Beltrán*, Félix. *About Design*. La Habana, Book Cuban Institute, 1975.
- *Bochenski*, I.M. *Current Methods of Thought*. 9a. ed., Madrid, Ediciones Rialp, 1974
- *Bonsiepe*, Gui. *Industrial Design, Technology and Dependence*. Mexico, Edicol. 1978
- *Bonsiepe*, Gui. *Theory and Practice of Industrial Design*. Barcelona, Ed. Gustavo Gili, 1978
- *Braunstein*, Néstor A. y otros. *Psychology, Ideology and Science*. 6a. ed., Mexico, Siglo XXI Eds., 1979.
- *Campi*, Isabel. Cit. in "Diseño, diseño: BCD Foundation" en *Magenta*, No. 4, Guadalajara, otoño, 1983
- *Carrillo*, Elba "Creativity" in *Educational Profiles*, No. 1, Mexico, CISE-UNAM, jul-ago-sept, 1978
- Cervo, Amado L. y Pedro Alcino Bervian. *Scientific Methodology*. Bogotá, Ed. Mc. Graw-Hill, 1980.

- *Cross*, Nigel and others. *Designing the Future*. Barcelona, Ed. Gustavo Gili, 1980
- *Del Palacio*, Alejandro. *Neoliberalism and revolution. Crisis and need for change.* 2ª Ed., Mexico, Latinoamerican Codes, 1995
- *Dondis*, D. A. *Image Syntax*. Barcelona, Gustavo Gili. 1976.
- *Duverger*, Maurice. *Social Sciences Methods*. 11a. ed. Barcelona, Ed. Ariel, 1980.
- *Eco*, Umberto. *How to do a Thesis*. 3a. ed. Mexico, Gedisa, 1982
- *Elliot*, David y Nigel Cross. *Design, Technology and Participation*. Barcelona, Ed. Gustavo Gili, 1980
- *Fernández* Alba, Antonio. "Process as Creative Action" in Jorge Sánchez de Antuñano (comp.). *Design Process*. Mexico. UAM, 1976
- *García* Olvera, Francisco. "Design Definition 1" in *Magenta*, No. 02, Guadalajara, primavera, 1983.
- *García* Olvera, Francisco. "Design Definition 2" in *Magenta*, No. 03, Guadalajara, verano, 1983.
- *Gortari*, Eli de. *General Methodology and Special Methods*. Ed. Océano, Barcelona, 1983.
- *Gutiérrez*, M.L. and others. *Against a dependent design*. Edicol, Mexico, 1977
- *Hanson*, Keith. "Design Based in Systems linked to Needings" in J. S. de Antuñano (comp.). *Design Process*. Mexico, UAM, 1976
- "Interview: DI Alejandro Lazo Margain" in *Magenta*, No. 01, Guadalajara, invierno, 1983.
- *Jones*, J. Christopher. *Design Methods*. Barcelona, Ed. Gustavo Gili, 1976
- *Karo*, Jerzy. *Graphic Design. Problems. Methods. Solutions.* New York, Van Nostrand Reinhold Co., 1975.
- *Kopnin*, P.V. *Dialectic Logics*. Mexico, Ed. Grijalbo, 1966
- *Kuhn*, Thomas. *Scientific Revolutions Structure*. Mexico, FCE, 1971.
- *Laurent*, Wolf. "Ideology and Production: The Design" in Mario A. Vázquez y José M. Gutiérrez (comps.). *Design User*. Mexico. UAM-Azcapotzalco, 1974
- *Linton*, Ralph. "Clasificaciones" in Patricia Ríos-Zertuche D. *The designer against designed*.. Mexico, UAM-Azcapotzalco, 1977.
- *Llovet*, Jordi. *Ideology and Design Methodology*. Barcelona, Ed. Gustavo Gili, 1979
- *Löbach*, Bernd. *Industrial Design*. Barcelona, Ed. Gustavo Gili, 1981
- *Maldonado*, Tomás. *Industrial Design Reconsidered*. Barcelona, Ed. Gustavo Gili, 1977
- *Maldonado*, Tomás. *Vanguard and Rationality*. Barcelona, E. Gustavo Gili, 1977.
- *Marx*, Carlos. "From epilogue to the second edition of Capital" in *Introduction to the Economy Critique /1857*. 9a. ed. Buenos Aires, Past and Present Papers, 1974.

- *Marx*, Carlos, *The Capital*. Vol. 1, 6a. reimp., Mexico, FCE, 1974.
- *Marx*, Carlos, *Feuerbach Thesis and other Phylosophical Writings*. Mexico, Ed. Grijalbo, 1970.
- *Moles*, Abraham, *The Objects* 2a. ed. Buenos Aires, Ed. Contemporary Time, 1974
- *Moles*, Abraham. *Objects Theory* 2a. ed. Barcelona, Ed. Gustavo Gili, 1975
- *Morris*, Charles. *Signs Theory Fundamentals*. Barcelona, Paidós Comunicación, 1994
- *Munari*, Bruno. *How do Objects are Born?* Barcelona, Ed. Gustavo Gili, 1983.
- *Munari*, Bruno. *Design and Visual Communication*. Barcelona, Ed. Gustavo Gili, 1974
- *Munari*, Bruno. *Art as a Craft*, 4a. ed. Barcelona, Ed. Labor, 1980
- *Olea*, Oscar y Carlos González Lobo. *Analysis and Logic Design*. Mexico, Ed. Trillas, 1977
- *Pando* Orellana, María. "Toward a more social approach to Design" in *Design Notebooks*, No. 1. Mexico, Iberoamerican University, mayo 1983.
- *Papanek*, Víctor. *Design for the Real World*. Madrid, H. Blume eds., 1973
- *Pardinas*, Felipe y otros. *General Model of Design Process*. Mexico, UAM-Azcapotzalco, 1975
- *Polya*, G. "How to solve a Problem" in J. Sánchez de Antuñano (comp.). *Design Process*. Mexico, UAM, n/d.
- *Popper*, Karl. *Scientific Researching Logic*. Madrid, Tecnos, 1973.
- *Prieto*, Daniel. *Design and Communication*. Mexico, UAM, 1982
- *Prieto* Castillo, Daniel. *Communication in Design and Education*. Mexico, UAM-Azcapotzalco, n/d.
- *Prieto* Castillo, Daniel. *Introduction to the Phantoms*. Mexico, UAM, n/d
- *Ricard*, André. *Design ¿Why?* Barcelona, Ed. Gustavo Gili, 1982
- *Rodríguez* Morales, Luis. "Semiotics and Design" in *Design Notebooks*, 1. Mexico, Iberoamerican University, 1983.
- *Rodríguez* Morales, Luis. "About Creativity" in *Design Notebooks*, 2. Mexico, Iberoamerican University, 1983.
- *Rubert* de Ventós, Xavier. "Applied art - Involved art" in Jorge Sánchez de Antuñano (comp.). *Design Process*. Mexico, UAM, n/d.
- *Rubert* de Ventós, Xavier. "Towards an integration of Art, Science and Technology: The Scientific Design" in J. Sánchez de Antuñano (comp.). *Design Process*. Mexico, UAM, 1979
- *Scott*, Gillam. *Design Fundamentals*. 13a. ed. Buenos Aires, Ed. Víctor Lerú, 1979
- *Selle*, G. *Ideology and Utopia of Design*. Barcelona, Ed. Gustavo Gili, 1973
- *Selltiz*, Claire y otros. "Researching Process" in *Social Sciences Methodology*. Mexico. ENEP-Acatlán, UNAM, 1978

- "Simón: Industrial Design Method" in *Magenta*, No. 04, Guadalajara, otoño, 1983.
- *Taylor*, Richard. *A basic course in graphic design*. New York, Van Nostrand Reinhold Co., 1971
- *Van Dijk*, Teun A. *Discourse Structures and Functions*. Mexico, Siglo XXI,1980.
- *Vilchis*, Luz del Carmen. *Design: Universe Knowledge*. Mexico, Centro Juan Acha AC/UNAM, 2002.
- *Williams*, Christopher. *Form Origins*. Barcelona, Ed. Gustavo Gili, 1983.
- *Wright*, Mills, C. *Sociological Imagination*. 6a. reimp. Mexico, FCE, 1977.

IMAGE CREDITS

1. *Theory. Library*, 2014, photography. Author: Luz del Carmen Vilchis
2. *Method. Relativity Formula*, 2014, photography. Author: Luz del Carmen Vilchis
3. *Organized Thought. Church Maps*, 2014, photography. Author: Luz del Carmen Vilchis
4. *Technique. Airbrush*, 2014, photography. Author: Luz del Carmen Vilchis
5. *Research. Searching for Knowledge*, (Books Author: Luz del Carmen Vilchis) 2014, photography. Author: Luz del Carmen Vilchis
6. *Reflection. Searching for Data*, 2014, photography. Author: Luz del Carmen Vilchis
7. *Abstraction and Synthesis. Confronting Knowledge*, 2014, photography. Author: Luz del Carmen Vilchis
8. *Knowledge. Setting the Knowledge*, 2014, photography. Author: Luz del Carmen Vilchis
9. *Thinking Frameworks. Design Methodology Diagram*. 2014, photography. Author: Luz del Carmen Vilchis
10. *Thinking Frameworks. Approach to Design Object Diagram*. 2014, photography. Author: Luz del Carmen Vilchis
11. *Thinking Frameworks. Design Process Diagram*. 2014, photography. Author: Luz del Carmen Vilchis
12. *Thinking Frameworks. Understanding Design Diagram*. 2014, photography. Author: Luz del Carmen Vilchis
13. *Problem. Fallen Roof*, 2014, photography. Author: Luz del Carmen Vilchis
14. *Project. "Varia Inventione" Book Cover (Design: Luz del Carmen Vilchis)*. 2014, photography. Author: Luz del Carmen Vilchis
15. *Solution. Manual Ladder*, 2014, photography. Author: Luz del Carmen Vilchis
16. *Parallel Solution. Folding Bench*, 2014, photography. Author: Luz del Carmen Vilchis

17. *Food Necessity. Alfeñique Fair in Mexico,* 2014, photography. Author: Luz del Carmen Vilchis
18. *Home Necessity. Bogota House,* 2014, photography. Author: Luz del Carmen Vilchis
19. *Transportation* Necessity. *Food stands trolleys,* 2014, photography. Author: Luz del Carmen Vilchis
20. *Ludic Necessity. Mexican "papier maché" Doll,* 2014, photography. Author: Luz del Carmen Vilchis
21. *Brand Necessity. Brand Nemontemi (Graphic Designer: Luz del Carmen Vilchis)* 2014, photography. Author: Luz del Carmen Vilchis
22. *Sign Necessity. Street Signs in Guatemala,* 2014, photography. Author: Luz del Carmen Vilchis
23. *Ornamentation* Necessity. *"El Pueblito Boyacense" in Colombia,* 2014, photography. Author: Luz del Carmen Vilchis
24. *Security Necessity. Metal Padlock,* 2014, photography. Author: Luz del Carmen Vilchis
25. *Casual User. Anonymus Custom,* 2014, photography. Author: Luz del Carmen Vilchis
26. *Functional User. Rulers,* 2014, photography. Author: Luz del Carmen Vilchis
27. *Independent User. Personal Bike,* 2014, photography. Author: Luz del Carmen Vilchis
28. *Colective User. Antigua Moto-taxi,* 2014, photography. Author: Luz del Carmen Vilchis
29. *Creativity. Folded bike,* 2014, photography. Author: Luz del Carmen Vilchis
30. *Fantasy. Mouse in the shape of ladybug,* 2014, photography. Author: Luz del Carmen Vilchis
31. *Invention. Dominican Mask,* 2014, photography. Author: Luz del Carmen Vilchis
32. Conscious Sense. *Plastic Toy,* 2014, photography. Author: Luz del Carmen Vilchis
33. *Practical Aspect. Foldable chairs,* 2014, photography. Author: Luz del Carmen Vilchis
34. *Practical Aspect. Félix Beltrán, CLIK Poster,* Habana, *1969* (public domain). López Hernández, Flor de Lis. Cuban Poster in RGB+K. *Design Information Magazine.* CONADICOV Archive License.
35. *Symbolic Aspect. Stapler,* 2014, photography. Author: Luz del Carmen Vilchis
36. *Symbolic Aspect. Spain Posters World 82* Official Program of World Soccer, Spain 82 (public domain). CONADICOV Archive License.
37. *Aesthetic Aspect. Chairs of the eighteenth century,* 2014, photography. Author: Luz del Carmen Vilchis

38. *Aesthetic Aspect.* Chris Kluge, *Musical Insects of the World.* Hitherto Unheralded Entomological Wonders! Nueva York, 1979. CONADICOV Archive License.
39. *Ludic Aspect. Wicker baskets toy*, 2014, photography. Author: Luz del Carmen Vilchis
40. *Ludic Aspect. Old Keys*, 2014, photography. Author: Luz del Carmen Vilchis
41. *Form-Function Variant. Ancient coal iron*, 2014, photography. Author: Luz del Carmen Vilchis
42. *Form-Function Variant. Trash cans for recycling*, 2014, photography. Author: Luz del Carmen Vilchis
43. *Form-Function Variant. Writing Objects*, 2014, photography. Author: Luz del Carmen Vilchis
44. *Form-Function Variant. Dices and Marbles*, 2014, photography. Author: Luz del Carmen Vilchis
45. *Syntax. Old Typewriter*, 2014, photography. Author: Luz del Carmen Vilchis
46. *Morphology. Garden Hose*, 2014, photography. Author: Luz del Carmen Vilchis
47. *Semantics. Pencil*, 2014, photography. Author: Luz del Carmen Vilchis
48. *Purpose. Dog House*, 2014, photography. Author: Luz del Carmen Vilchis
49. *Use Value. Bike*, 2014, photography. Author: Luz del Carmen Vilchis
50. *Symbolic Value. Smiling Clothes Hanger*, 2014, photography. Author: Luz del Carmen Vilchis
51. *Sign Value. Old sewing machine*, 2014, photography. Author: Luz del Carmen Vilchis
52. *Change Value. Bronze bookcases*, 2014, photography. Author: Luz del Carmen Vilchis
53. *Sense. Actual Keys*, 2014, photography. Author: Luz del Carmen Vilchis
54. *Sense. Cordless Phone*, 2014, photography. Author: Luz del Carmen Vilchis
55. *Function and intention. Wooden Match*, 2014, photography. Author: Luz del Carmen Vilchis
56. *Function and intention. Electric Switch*, 2014, photography. Author: Luz del Carmen Vilchis
57. *Bruno Munari Model Flowchart.* Author Free Translation. *http://www.arteac.edu.mx/libros/metodologia_del_disenio-fundamentos_teoricos.pdf*
58. *Papanek Model Flowchart.* Author Free Translation. *http://www.arteac.edu.mx/libros/metodologia_del_disenio-fundamentos_teoricos.pdf*
59. *Papanek Model Flowchart.* Author Free Translation. *http://www.arteac.edu.mx/libros/metodologia_del_disenio-fundamentos_teoricos.pdf*
60. *Jones Model Flowchart.* Author Free Translation. *http://www.arteac.edu.mx/libros/metodologia_del_disenio-fundamentos_teoricos.pdf*

61. *Jones Model Flowchart.* Author Free Translation. *http://www.arteac.edu.mx/libros/metodologia_del_disenio-fundamentos_teoricos.pdf*
62. *Löbach Model Flowchart.* Author Free Translation. *http://www.arteac.edu.mx/libros/metodologia_del_disenio-fundamentos_teoricos.pdf*
63. *Löbach Model Flowchart.* Author Free Translation. *http://www.arteac.edu.mx/libros/metodologia_del_disenio-fundamentos_teoricos.pdf*
64. *Moles Model Flowchart.* Author Free Translation. *http://www.arteac.edu.mx/libros/metodologia_del_disenio-fundamentos_teoricos.pdf*
65. *Moles Model Flowchart.* Author Free Translation. *http://www.arteac.edu.mx/libros/metodologia_del_disenio-fundamentos_teoricos.pdf*
66. *Bonsiepe Model Flowchart.* Author Free Translation. *http://www.arteac.edu.mx/libros/metodologia_del_disenio-fundamentos_teoricos.pdf*
67. *Llovet Model Flowchart.* Author Free Translation. *http://www.arteac.edu.mx/libros/metodologia_del_disenio-fundamentos_teoricos.pdf*
68. *Olea Model Flowchart.* Author Free Translation. *http://www.arteac.edu.mx/libros/metodologia_del_disenio-fundamentos_teoricos.pdf*
69. *UAM Model Flowchart.* Author Free Translation. *http://www.arteac.edu.mx/libros/metodologia_del_disenio-fundamentos_teoricos.pdf*
70. *Alexander Model Flowchart.* Author Free Translation. *http://www.arteac.edu.mx/libros/metodologia_del_disenio-fundamentos_teoricos.pdf*
71. *Vilchis Model Flowchart.* Author Free Translation. *L.C. Vilchis. Diseño. Universo de Conocimiento. Claves Latinoamericanas/UNAM, 2000*
72. *Vilchis Model Flowchart.* Author Free Translation. *L.C. Vilchis. Diseño. Universo de Conocimiento. Claves Latinoamericanas/UNAM, 2000*